T0381229

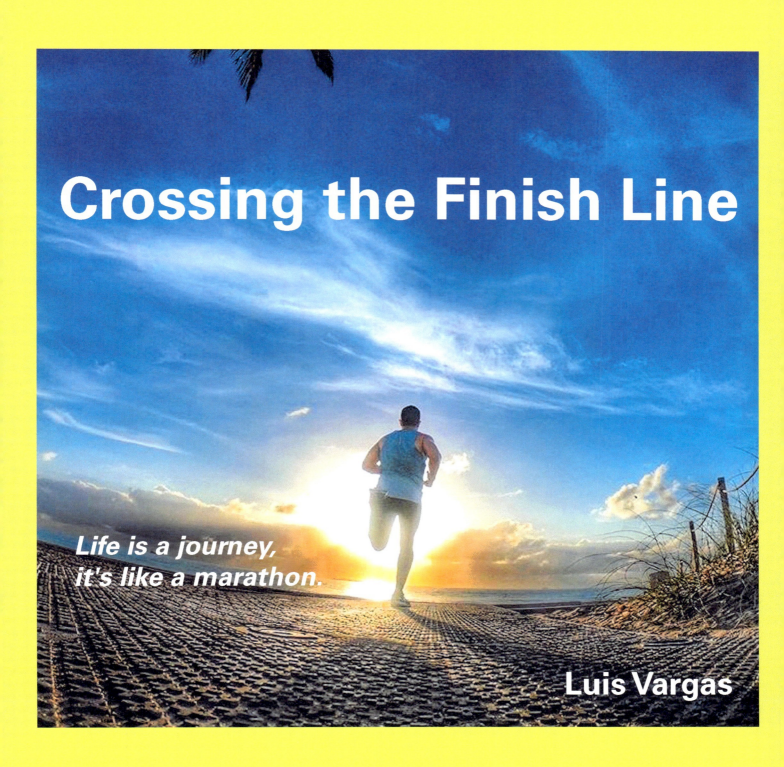

Crossing the Finish Line

*Life is a journey,
it's like a marathon.*

Luis Vargas

Crossing the Finish Line

iUniverse books may be ordered through booksellers or by contacting:

iUniverse
1663 Liberty Drive
Bloomington, IN 47403
www.iuniverse.com
1-800-Authors (1-800-288-4677)

ISBN: 978-1-5320-8216-0 (sc)
ISBN: 978-1-5320-8218-4 (hc)
ISBN: 978-1-5320-8217-7 (e)

Library of Congress Control Number: 2019913511

Print information available on the last page.

iUniverse rev. date: 09/16/2019

Crossing the Finish Line

Life is a series of ups and downs. Some ups come with joy and happiness. Some downs come with tears, pain and disappointment.
It's like a Marathon, some ups and some downs.

Contents

CROSSING THE FINISH LINE

Dedication

I dedicate this book to "Friends in Training" (FIT) for pouring out love and dedication to me, and many others. People of FIT, with hard work has offered motivation and support to hundreds of runners, improving their lives, taking on challenges, crossing with them the finish line. Friends in Training is one of the largest running clubs in South Florida. For more than 20 years, FIT has brought physical and mental health to many runners and walkers of all ages.

Acknowledgements

I want to give thanks to Luis Aguilar, Marisa Markowicz, Christina Quadra, Adrian Gandara, Jose Yamamoto, Veronica Rodriguez, Maria Beatriz Maiello de Krstonosic, Madeline Proano, for their contribution and for allow me to share about their own stories, stories of passion, commitment, determination and resilience. You are winners.

Thanks to Alexandra Ardila and her organization Biblio-Bicicleta, Ernie Tanner and his organization Helimission, and Dr. John Sherman and his organization CHIA Christian Hands in Action, for allowing me to share about their work with remote communities and their passion that has marked their race in life. You have put the lives of others in front of your own life. You are Champions.

My gratitude to all the friends of FIT, South Florida Runners, Pura Vida Run Club, iRun Company, Weston Run Club and 1,000 Miles Run Club for sharing many miles along roads, paths, parks, and bridges in all kinds of races with me. You are victorious.

Special acknowledgements to Marcela Todd, Ana Maria Villegas, and Luis Tovar for sharing their wisdom, talents, and motivation with me. You have worked hard to achieve many goals but in doing so, you always encourage others to be better and to reach their own goals. You are inspiration.

I am grateful to my kids David, Faith and Grace, the reason for my existence, for their constant encouragement. David you can destroy any giant on your way, raise up to be a king. Faith, you can believe in achieving the impossible and if you do, you'll do it. Grace, you have a special touch from God, a loving character that will allow you to develop your full potential. You are warriors.

My infinite gratitude to God, for giving me a second a third and many chances every day. You have created me, lived and died for me. You have been my coach, my inspiration, my support and my running partner. You have created my race. You have been my path and you are my finish line. You are awesome.

The greatest runs are moments in time that allow you to see how wonderful life is.

Friends in Training

"I did it" I surprise myself. I wasn't sure I could hold it until the end but I did it. So much effort, so much pain but so much love for what I do.

Ana Maria Villegas

Photo by Ana Maria Villegas

My day starts at night. I used to love sleeping and exercising was my New Year's resolution every single year, but everything changed when I discovered that running was my thing.

Ana Maria Villegas

INTRODUCTION

New York City, a beautiful city, a place that brings music to my mind, "A Heart in New York", "New York Groove", "New York State of Mind", and Frank Sinatra with his "New York, New York". A place that brings smells to my mind, pretzels, a hot slice of New York pizza, ice cream, and Chinese food from China Town. New York, a place that brings great sights to my mind, the Jets, the Yankees, the Macy's parade, New Year's Eve countdown, the Statute of Liberty, and of course, Fifth Avenue, the most expensive street in the world. I have seen parades on the Avenue. I have seen the Avenue in movies. I have seen Christmas decorations on the Avenue. But this time the Avenue looked different; I was in the middle of the Avenue running towards Central Park with more than 53,000 runners. The sky was blue and the bright sun was gleaming yellow. The leaves were bursting with autumn colors of red and brown, making Fifth Avenue look like a street of honor leading to the finish line, something I trained so hard for.

I made it – I crossed the finish line! I completed one of the greatest races in the world, the New York City Marathon. I looked around and I saw runners crossing the line, some lifting their arms, some crying, others jumping, each one of them carrying their own story. Stories of sacrifice, determination, and persistence. Now, I want to share with you my story, the story of winners I know, and how we overcame the setbacks life had thrown at us.

Have you ever thought about your race in life and where your journey is taking you? Where did you come from and where are you going? Life is a journey. And like a marathon, it's filled with hard moments that drain your strength. Yet, there are moments where you're so excited and joyful that you can't contain your happiness. You dance, you cry, you laugh, you are in pain, you feel proud of your love ones, or sad for a loss. I found it interesting comparing life with a marathon through the story of my friends and normal individuals that God has brought into my life. Dream facilitators and motivators who influence people and create an environment of positivity wherever they go. These are the people that see the glass half-full and not half-empty in the middle of tough situations.

After finishing the last curve in Central Park, I crossed the finish line. And even though I could barely walk, I was excited to see my medal was waiting for me. Only 1% of the American population run a marathon, and only 1% of them run the New York Marathon. It's an incredible feeling to be one of them, so I wear my medal with pride. Yet as I started walking, I had such pain on my hamstrings. It wasn't a pain of cramp, but a pain of effort. I stopped for a second and bent over to massage my muscles and try to relieve the feeling. Two paramedics approached me, gave me pain medicine, and guided me to the Red Cross tent. They made me lay down in one of many aligned beds. A physical therapist, gave me a massage and I was ready to keep going. In the race we call life, sometimes we have moments of pain, we need to stop, recover, heal, and keep pushing forward. We are not going back, we are just taking a pause, regrouping, and regaining strength.

Have you seen the picture of a monkey that starts walking and is being transformed step-by-step until becomes a man; one of those "evolution" pictures? Well, I felt like that. I left the tent with a bag of ice on my knee, a fresh massage on my legs, and began walking slowly. It's amazing how the body recovers. As I walked to the hotel, my body was getting back in shape, the pain gradually left, and I started walking normal. Within a couple of hours, I had to pack my bags, head to the airport, fly to South Carolina, and be ready to work the next day. When I woke up the next day, I was functioning even better than before and was toting the satisfaction that I accomplished something that looked impossible before.

When I made the last turn to enter Central Park, excitement filled my heart. I was few yards from the finish line. I finished with a time of 3:48, a personal record. That's not too bad, considering only three years before I wasn't able to run even three miles. At that time, I was crowned the winner for the biggest belly in the class reunion of the Colombian Air Force. I have made some progress, but the progress wasn't overnight. It was an accumulation of small changes, of constant training, and small daily decisions. The reward for those small decisions is great: It's a compound effect. We are product of small changes and decisions that happen in our lives, day after day. That's why we need to keep our daily priorities and set daily goals.

The last 800 meters of the race were strenuous, my heart was strong, and even though my legs didn't respond, they were burning. The words that came to my mind were, "Run the first 3/4 of the race with your head, and the last 1/4 of the race with your heart." That's where the real changes happen; in your head and in your mind. Every thought has a consequence, so you need to listen to your heart and follow your guts. I knew I had to fight. My legs wanted to give up on me, but I was not going to let them. I ordered my arms to swing forcefully and to activate those legs. If I was going to die, I was going to do it after the finish line, not before.

Life is not a sprint, it's a marathon. This book compares a marathon with life and it should offer a message of hope and personal development for you, even if you don't run. Sometimes you feel like you had to push your way to the top. You saved, you worked hard, and things looked like they were going in the right direction. But sometimes life takes a turn on you. Maybe you got some unexpected news, laid off, a contract that was cancelled, or a health issue, and now you are moving downhill. Like life, this famous marathon has its ups and downs. The last half of the NYC marathon was a constantly uphill, so it's difficult to see with your eyes where the finish line is. You can feel the effects all over, sometimes things start deteriorating, and when you realize they are different, it's too late. You see yourself and say, "What happened? How did I get here?"

New York is considered a hard race because of the ups and downs of the bridges. The Queensboro bridge on mile 16, and it was the one that almost killed me. I was maintaining a great pace of 8 minutes per mile, but by the time I left the bridge, it was down to 11. It was a hard and long climb; I had to push my body and my mind, even though I wasn't certain I'd make it.

We left Queensboro and turned to the bridge. We ran on the first deck of the bridge and it was silent. We could only listen the noise of the shoes pounding on the asphalt. We had to climb and climb, and it felt like we were almost not going to finish. Sometimes we face those situations in life that look like they are going last forever, like if they never are going to finish. But it's critical to remember that everything has a season. After the cold winter where there are no leaves on the trees, spring comes, offering new life, new flowers, and new foliage. If you are in the middle of your winter, take heart, your spring will come.

When we got to the top of the bridge, it felt like we had won the race right there. And then, the way down, it was relaxing and emotional. Suddenly, we could hear the cheers of the crowd again, see the smiles of the people, and hear the music of the bands playing; what a wonderful sight. Life is like that, if you don't have ups and downs, then it's because you're like a dead man walking. Just few years ago I was living like a zombie, like many live today. I was just shuffling back and forth from home, to work, back home, watching the same television programs, sitting in the same chair. Just to repeat the same thing over the next day. Now, I am full of life with a bright future full of dreams and aspirations. I want to share with you how change came to my life and hopefully inspire and motivate you to be the best version of yourself.

Have you ever wondered what you can compare to your journey in life? I have a friend, Rodrigo, who just finished his MBA. His effort and dedication reminded me of the same I had to put into my journey in life. He said the best comparison he had with completing his MBA is with a marathon. You need perseverance, consistency, have the mind on the goal, and hold on during the last few miles.

Before the Queensboro bridge, we were in Queensborough. It was so full of people from many backgrounds and nationalities cheering us on. Life was good; it was like auto pilot was engaged. My pace was good, I was comfortable, I didn't expect things were going to change at the Queensboro bridge. Sometimes everything is working fine, everything looks in place, and the routine is normal. There are no worries, but not all things turn out the way we want. A short sale, a relationship that turn out bad, sickness creeped on the family. What do we do? Keep moving forward. Don't give up and trust in God. When things are going well, enjoy it, enjoy every moment, every second. Enjoy the sunrise, the sun, the park, enjoy your children, your friends, enjoy what you like to do. Have fun, live in the here and now. But when things change and suddenly your road takes a new direction, and there is an obstacle in front of you, like a high bridge, take courage, trust in God and keep going. After every storm the calm will come, the light will shine at the end of the tunnel.

Brooklyn Borough, was one part of the race that I really enjoyed. I ran by the people and raised my hands to make them cheer for me. I didn't know them, but their energy gave me energy. If you have energy, give good energy. What you give you will get in return, if you give a smile, you will get a smile, if you give love, you will get love. You reap what you sow.

The best photo I have seen of the New York Marathon is an aerial picture over the Verrazano-Narrows bridge, showing the bridge full or runners as they crossed the first two miles of the race. In contrast with Queensboro bridge at mile 16, this is a bridge to enjoy. The ascend is easy but the descend tries to trick you; if you don't hold the pace, you end up going too fast without noticing. Sometimes we go too fast, we need to slow down, we make decisions quickly, we want things quickly, and we want results quickly. The antidote to this is patience. Have you ever had taken a short cut in life because you think that is going to get you there quicker, and then you find out that it was worse than you hoped? One of the biggest things in my life, and that I am still learning, is to slow down. Somehow, we think that being busy is being productive. We try to get some quality time with our family and friends and we find these words in the way, "Sorry, I am too busy, we'll do it later." It's like people want to look more important or more professional because they are busier. There is much to be learned from Japanese people; they like to slow down. If you have a meeting with Japanese business men, you might find irritated at how they look like they're going to sleep while making decisions. They think about it, meditate on it, evaluate, and listen to their hearts. On the contrary, we see people making split-second decisions and rushing. Take your time, enjoy your meal, enjoy your company, enjoy the sun, the walk, the nature or the buildings. Enjoy everything.

Before Verrazano bridge, was the start. The expectations, the preparation; this is it! It turned out to be a beautiful day, the race was ahead, but I felt like I had already won. The moment I pressed the button on my watch and I made the first step over the start line, I won. I didn't think about the 26.2 miles ahead. I didn't think about my legs giving up. I just did it, I took the first step, and I was moving forward.

The night before the race I was on the ferry to Staten Island, the water at night shined with the full moon and the view of the Statute of Liberty was breath taking.; this is one of my favorite sights of New York. This was my third major global marathon. Just two weeks before the New York Marathon, I ran the Chicago Marathon, and the year before I ran my first major in Berlin. I've seen many beautiful sights; New York with the Statue of Liberty, a landmark that means freedom, Berlin with the wall, a landmark that means captivity. I have my freedom and it's priceless, I can't complain. I am healthy, better than millions of people with only one week left to live. There is food on my table. I have clothes. A bed to sleep in and a roof over my head. I am wealthier than 75% of the world. We need to look at the glass half-full, not half-empty. We need to change the way we look at things. That is freedom and liberty. I am created equal. I am endowed by my Creator with the right of life, liberty, and pursuit of happiness, something that the Declaration of Independence says. It is what I declare in my life every day.

The ferry to Staten Island is free. For many people, this means the opportunity to do something exciting, to discover new things, and a way to enjoy their freedom. For others could be just another boring ride to go to their boring job that maybe can't stand, could be the way to go back home where a daily fight is waiting, a way to their captivity. For me, it was a way to connect the past in captivity with the present in freedom, a way to enjoy freedom and to remember where I came from. A way to connect my third world major marathon in New York and the statue of liberty that stands for freedom with my first world major in Berlin and the wall, a memory of captivity. Let me share with you my journey from captivity to liberty, from the wall of captivity to the torch of liberty...

Running is not about being better than someone else. It's about being better than you used to be.

Luis Tovar

Photo by Luis Tovar

Running has taught me to be patient and smart. It might not happen in your time but will happen in the right time. Rushing and pushing too much can only hurt you.

Ana Maria Villegas

Photo by Ana Maria Villegas

My biggest fear in running used to be a bad race or even a failed workout. But with time I learned failure is inevitable, but don't let it get to your heart. Learn and use it as fuel for the next one.

Ana Maria Villegas

Photo by Ana Maria Villegas

Chapter 1.
THE BASE

Motivation

When I lived in Miami in 1992, I experienced first-hand the force of Hurricane Andrew. I was living with some friends from Spain, and we decided to stay in the house to ride it out. The noise and the shaking were as if a train was passing by right next to the house. We heard the noise of trees falling over houses, and then suddenly, a period of calm and a blue sky came. It was the eye of the hurricane. We went outside, and what we saw around us was painful—so many houses were destroyed. Everyone's lives changed in one day.

Many building codes were changed for the new homes in Florida due to Hurricane Andrew, making the foundation and structure of the houses stronger to resist hurricanes.

In coastal Louisiana, houses are built over pilings to keep the buildings above flood waters. They are the base of the house and provide support, but if one of those pilings is broken or missing, the whole house is compromised. It is like a table that needs four legs to stand.

In life, we need strong frames and a strong foundation in six different areas: fitness, health, relationships, spirituality, economy, and nutrition. We find balance in our lives if those foundations are strong, but if one of those fails, we won't live our lives to their maximum potential.

True motivation is when you find your purpose in life, or the reason you were created. If you know your purpose in life, then it will be your motivation for all six areas of your life.

We live in abundance when we live in the place where purpose, talents, and helping others cross roads. When we live in that place, we can set up our priorities of health, time, spirit, provision, and relationships as they orbit around your purpose. If I understand what my purpose is, I can be around people who identify with my purpose, I can organize my time according to my purpose, I can be proactive so that my body can allow me to accomplish my purpose, and I can feed my spirit to discern, to have peace, and be of sound mind for my purpose.

One day, my friend Luis, was spending time with his children. They were out in the park trying the new bikes with training wheels that he got for them. He felt sad to see that because of his physical condition; he was not able to keep up with the kids. When he tried to run holding his son's bike as he was trying to pedal by himself, he saw himself short of breath, tired, and slow because of his physical condition. In that moment, he decided to change. His motivation was his children, his purpose in life. Now, Luis is an amazing runner. He is strong and completed his first marathon in 4 hours. He ran his second marathon only two weeks after the first one. We worked together to build his base, and to add volume and speed to his running. It required many hours of training, but we couldn't do that if it wasn't for his motivation.

Initially, my motivation was to have energy, lose weight, release stress, and be a better person in every area of my life. I wanted to be successful. Now my motivation is to help as many people as I can with my talents. I make goals, and as I accomplished them, I make more goals. They may be goals in different areas of life or within the same. One of those goals I made was to run the six major marathons of the world, and that started in Berlin.

On that September morning of 2017, I woke up to put on the gear that I had laid out the night before. I opened the curtains and saw the streets of Berlin covered with a light drizzle; the temperature, even on the cold side, was perfect for the race. The streets were dressed up with beautiful decorations, signs for the Berlin Marathon, and mingling about were other signs for political candidates that were going to be elected the same day. This was the first time I was going to run in one of the six major world marathons. While I still had other cities to hit like Chicago, New York, London, Tokyo, Berlin, it was the beginning of a dream that eventually will be accomplished.

Before leaving the hotel to go to the race, I met with my group. They were people mainly from Spain, but others were from Peru, Colombia, the USA, the Netherlands, the Dominican Republic, and Brazil. The day before, we all wore the colors of our countries at the parade of nations in the Olympic stadium of Berlin. I was amazed when I saw the multitude of colors in harmony. It was incredible that this was the same place where the African American super star, Jesse Owens, won his four gold medals in the face of Hitler, including the 4x100 relay with his outstanding 39.8 seconds, a record that he held for 20 years. So much racial division was evident in the 1930s, but now we were running together – running like brothers. When Jesse ran, he felt freedom. For him, it was not important if someone was different from another. The only important thing was to win; for me, although winning is a great accomplishment, there is more to winning than obtaining first place. So, what is winning? Is it to break the world record? To break your own record? To get out and decide to participate? To cross the finish line? What is wining and, more importantly, what is success? I believe success is to live life at your full potential. To find your purpose, your life project. To find the reason why you are in this world and your passion and to live it, that is the main motivation to get up every day, to eat better, to run or do whatever is your passion, to help people, to be closer to our creator, the same one that put that purpose in our hearts.

Life is worth living when you find your purpose. When you don't know what it is, and everybody is telling you what to do, and you don't know what to believe, follow your heart. Mark Twain said, "The two most important days in your life are the day you were born and the day you found out why." In the classic Christmas movie "It's a wonderful life", George Bailey discovers how life would be without him, he realizes that he is part of many peoples' lives. His contribution was his purpose. Even if you touch one life, that person my influence others who can, in turn, influence many others.

Jesse Owens broke the world record, and that was a great success, but he also started a friendship with the best athlete of Germany, his competitor Lutz Long. They displayed gestures of sportsmanship, friendship, and empathy during the Olympic games of 1936, in spite of criticism and the pressure of the Nazi regime over Lutz. That friendship was a success. Lutz helped Jesse qualify for the long jump. When he saw that Jesse had problems clearing the white line, Lutz gave Jesse a tip to try something different. In his third and final attempt, Jesse saw Lutz putting a white cloth one step before the white line to show Jesse where his new mark was. Then, he stayed there to see Jesse make the jump and qualify for the gold medal competition. When Lutz saw Jesse making the winning jump, he ran to congratulate Jesse and put his arms around him. What Lutz did was incredible; it was an act of generosity and kindness. To be happy for his competitor, in the middle of the greatest event, in times of political tension and discrimination, that is success.

God created us all equal and he allows us to run side by side. We all have our own race, but we can run it together. Something remarkable about FIT is that they embrace diversity regardless of age, fitness level, or gender. Anyone can join FIT and be part of a community that helps and celebrate each other. I shared the race in Berlin with some friends from FIT. I was very happy to meet people from all over the world running in the same event. The 2017 Berlin Marathon had 43,852 participants from all around the world who all prepared for more than three months. They all got up early to run miles and miles, three, four, or five days a week. They were all converging in the same place, waving hands to the sound of Brazilian music and counting down: Ten, nine, eight, seven, six, five, four, three, two, one… GO!

Our hotel was just few blocks from Checkpoint Charlie, an entrance to the famous Berlin Wall, the crossing point between East Berlin and West Berlin during the Cold War. We left the hotel and passed by a remaining piece of the Berlin Wall. My heart ached at the thought of the people that tried to escape to the West in order to recover their liberty. The most beautiful gift from God is freedom. So many sacrifices and high prices are paid for us to enjoy it. Walking the streets of Berlin and seeing the contrast between the past and the present filled my heart with gratitude for the freedom that I enjoy. I am free to worship, to make my own decisions, and to pursue happiness.

We headed to Brandenburg Gate, where Ronald Regan gave the famous speech "Tear Down this Wall." He called the leader of the Soviet Union, Mikhail Gorbachev, to open up the barrier that had divided West and East Berlin since 1961, marking a new era of change. The Berlin Wall kept change out for many years, but that forced people to be creative in finding ways to escape. We have walls in our own lives and that keep us from change, but we can tear down those walls with creativity and faith. Sometimes, the only way people become creative is when they hit a wall. They may feel like the wall won't break. They can either resign and do nothing, becoming conformists, or they can find ways to break the wall. The walls are there and it is painful to break them, but if we want to reinvent ourselves, we need to deal with the pain and keep trying to break it. Eventually the walls will fall. God gave us the strength to find the cracks, to penetrate the walls, and to break them. It is great when we find motivation from our success and we want to build on that, but sometimes we need to find motivation from the hard situations in life. We might see a wall around us, but we need to keep pressing on until we break the wall. We need to find motivation in our problems. Problems are not problems, they are opportunities.

At the Brandenburg Gate, John F. Kennedy also gave his famous speech "Ich bin ein Berliner", meaning "I am a Berliner." I felt like a Berliner, I identified with the people of Berlin. Berlin is such a wonderful city with a sporty and healthy lifestyle. The day before the main race, hundreds of kids ran The Bambino Marathon. The inline skating marathon also took place. It was amazing to see the groups of skaters pressing on to get to the finish line, some of them with bruises. I saw a man with his face covered in blood after he fell, but he kept going. What gave him strength to finish after such an injury? It could only be tenacity, determination, and self-motivation. No matter how difficult the race can be, no matter how difficult the problem is, we need to keep going and never give up. Like my daughters say, "The grind never stops", so keep on grinding. We keep moving forward until the end. Martin Luther King said, "If you can't fly, then run. If you can't run, then walk. If you can't walk, then crawl. But whatever you do, you have to keep moving forward".

The statue of four horses pulling the chariot of the goddess of Victory, the Quadriga, over the Brandenburg gate was a witness of many world events. Now, it is a witness of thousands of marathoners' achievements. It was a witness of the change of coach Luis, who has helped many like me to believe in themselves. When Luis went to the Berlin Marathon, he crossed the gate at the end of the race. He was crying, and had been crying since kilometer 35. He was not crying of pain but crying of excitement of what that accomplishment meant to him. It was a change that started a few years before. When he crossed the Brandenburg gate, he had the assurance that he was going to cross the finish line under the six hours allowed by the race. He had to walk the whole race as he was recovering from three fractured vertebras caused by osteopenia. He had to have two surgeries to reconstruct his tendons, and had another surgery on his left leg to treat his meniscus. He never left his faith or his purpose. Berlin was a mark of many pains left behind and new dreams ahead. For him, life is like a marathon and not all the marathons are the same, each Marathon has its particularities, some with many ups and downs, others with many curves. Each mile is different. The Berlin Marathon was special because he saw the closing of a painful chapter. It is like we read in Ecclesiastes, everything has its place and its time. A marathon can give us the discipline that we need to cope with the change, and give us structure. In life sometimes, we need to have patience and have a steady pace, other times we need to go faster, to be consistent, and have purpose. The beautiful thing about a marathon is that you can set a goal and reach the goal you planned. You train for what you want to do and then you do for what you have trained. We pilots say, you plan your flight, and then you fly your plan.

The change in Luis' life started when he left a busy life with work. Between 25 and 35 years old, he went through a difficult time in his life. When he was 36, he moved to Costa Rica as he felt God wanted him to do something different. So, Luis began to look for Him, and tried to live a healthier life and find balance. Then when he moved to the US, he had an encounter with God. He felt that his life needed to include a big change including exercise. He started walking, 30 to 45 minutes. As soon as he began, the physical, emotional, and spiritual healing started to take place. Then, he started running. After being invited by a friend to run a 5K, he liked it so much he decided to become a runner. He created new habits, as he now understood that our body is God's temple and we are responsible to take care of it. What started like a hobby turned into a discipline. The fact that he had a spiritual change and that he found a way to bring body and Spirit in tune, the fact of having a medical need to clean and reduce weight and the need to find a healthy balance gave him the motivation to what he considers is more than a lifestyle, a change witnessed by the Quadriga of the Brandenburg Gate.

The Quadriga was also witness of the change in my life that started two years before the race when certain events affected the way I was living. I found myself out of balance. I was living like a zombie, emotionally devastated, and scoring low in health, self-esteem, and motivation. I could barely run three miles, and sometimes I saw myself a failure. Wait a minute! That was two years before the race, that was the way I was looking at myself, with my own eyes, it was not the way God looked at me with his eyes. In God's eyes I am a perfect creation, he made me wonderfully and fearfully, I have been made in His image. When I saw myself as a person that could barely run three miles, God saw me like a marathoner. Sometimes we see ourselves as only able to run a short distance, but God create us to run much farther distances. God created us to be like eagles and to fly high. Eagles that can soar above the storm, with a vision to enlarge their territories. That is who I really am, I am healthy, my body is strong, I am professional, I am interesting, and I was created in the image of God. I have dreams given by God, I take risks, and I am confident. I can do things that look impossible, but with God nothing is impossible. That is the way God sees me, and sees you, with love. I am not a superstar but he still loves me. He loves me with such love that he gave his own son to die for me and for you.

Personal Inventory

Now that you have made the decision, you are motivated, and you have your goal in mind, it's time to grab a pen and start writing. Where are you and where do you want to go? If you want to become debt free, you need to start writing down everything you spend. If you want to eat healthier, you need to write everything down you are eating. If you want to exercise more and be healthier, you need to write everything down that you are doing to move your body. You need to write how you are using your time and what kind of thoughts are you thinking. If you are having negative thoughts about yourself, write all the good things that you are. When you see things in paper you can see what things you need to improve, change, or eliminate.

Write your goals, at least your ten main goals. From your ten most important goals, prioritize and select the three most important goals. Then from those three, select one. That is your number one goal, that is your One Thing. Work on that, and then the next. Gary Keller in his book "The One Thing" (1) (Keller, 2013) describes how this One Thing can be the most important thing in your life, or for this month, or this week, or for today. He asked the question "What is the one thing that you can do this week such that by doing it everything else would be easier or unnecessary?" If you focus on that One Thing today will have impact in what you do tomorrow or for the rest of your life. It is like a domino effect, if you push one domino piece, that piece will release a small amount of energy that will start a chain of reactions in a row of pieces as they start falling one by one. In other words, by doing this small action, it will facilitate a bigger action that will facilitate an even bigger action. If you have 4,491,863 dominos in line close to each other, one single amount of energy is enough to tilt one to fall onto another domino, and then another, creating a chain reaction that results in the falling of almost 4.5 million dominos. One single amount of energy released a cumulative force of 94,000 joules. Same energy that will take a man to complete 545 pushups. But supposed that the second domino is double the size of the first one, and the third is double the size of the second and so on. This progression was studied by Dr. Whitehead, a physicist. He proved that if the first domino was two inches long, the 10th domino would be the size of a football player, and the 18th domino the size of the Leaning Tower of Pisa. The energy that you put in your One Thing for this day will have an exponential impact in the One Thing of your life. This is why it's important to put it in your daily schedule. Make it a point to carve out time to work on your dream, your life project. You can work for somebody else, but this time is to work for yourself.

One of the secrets to start running consistently is to start where you are. To take a personal inventory. If we know where we are, we can focus on where to start. Sometimes we set goals too high to achieve and we overthink that if we start hard, fast and long, we can get to that goal faster. But if you don't have the base mileage and try to push yourself too much too fast, it's only a matter of time before you end in pain. Dr. Phillip Maffetone, who developed the Maffetone Method (2) (Maffeone, 2000), is a believer that the days of "no pain no gain" are over. The Maffetone method focus on three areas:

nutrition, exercise and maximum aerobic function. In my opinion, it's the best method to develop an aerobic base. With your training you need to set a realistic goal. If you have only three days a week available for training, then find a plan that fits that time. Also, you need to set realistic goals for your race distance and time. In my first marathon, my goal was just to finish, not with a specific finish time in mind. It was just to relax and enjoy the race. I took pictures, waited in lines for the bathroom, and "walked run". I trained for a 5:15 race, and even though I finished at 5:25, I was satisfied that I achieved my goal to finish. In the marathon of life, you need to set yourself up for success, not for failure. Start with small goals and build on those.

When I started running, I was about 30 pounds over my optimal weight. I was running like carrying a backpack containing 30 pounds of rocks. When I lost those 30 pounds, I felt like I didn't have to run anymore carrying that backpack full of rocks. It was a heavy burden and that burden was part of my inventory. We carry many heavy burdens. Perhaps it's garbage that we collect from the past. But once I surrendered my life to Jesus and gave my burdens to him, I let him carry my backpack full of rocks of remorse, guilt, shame, and worry. I gave all my problems to Him and He let me rest. I was at peace. I was running my race through the valley of death, but I was holding his hand, and when the time to rest came, it was like when a sheep lays in green pastures resting because the shepherd is taking care of him. I know the voice of my shepherd. He refreshes my soul. I lack nothing.

My son's name remains me of two characters: King David because he can fight any giant, and Christian, from the book "The Pilgrim's Progress" of John Bunyan (3) (Bunyan, 1967). In the book, Christian started a journey, a race, from the City of Destruction to the Celestial City. Christian carries a heavy burden through the walk of life until he ventures to the place of deliverance. There, the Lord takes his burdens away. He had to cross the Wicked Gate, go through the Hill of Difficulty, the Valley of Humiliation, the Fearful Valley, the City of Destruction, and Vanity Fair. His friend, Hopeful, helped him to get out of the Castle of Doubtfulness with the keys of Promise that opened the door for them to escape. Finally, they reached the finish line at the Celestial City after the burden was taken away. If you have to carry a burden, that is ok, it is your personal inventory, but you can find your place of deliverance and leave your burden there.

There was definitely a gap between how I looked at myself and how God looked at me. There was a gap and to close the gap, I needed to change. We are all resistant to change. For me, change required a commitment to create new habits, but what really meant was to change the way of thinking. Our brain is very lazy, resistant to change, and tries to push us into our comfort zone. We need to try to get out of that comfort zone, because only out of it can we see great things happen. Only there is where we can develop our potential and see growth in our lives. Small races, 5K, 10k, or half marathons are races that can be demanding, but they are not going to take you out of your comfort zone. The distance of a marathon, 26.2 miles, is a beautiful distance that always will push you. Your brain will tell your body to stop, to go and rest, and you will fight with your will and your mind. Only when we are outside of the box we can raise over the storm, like the eagle that uses the storm winds to be lifted over the same storm and fly over it. We can fly higher with resilience. We may have all kinds of problems, and I know that the problem can be big, but God is bigger than those problems and we can rest on him. By resting on him, we can soar.

That was my reality. I started running three miles, and when I started with group C, I was able to run 5 miles; my pace was about 11:30. My fitness condition and my reality was that I was overweight. My eating habits were not the best. I went through a divorce. My business was slow. My financial situation was deteriorating and my spirit was hurt. That was my personal inventory. I needed to change, I needed to reinvent myself, start again, and be a new creation. Before we start making changes, we need to do a personal inventory of how things are going. Be candid with yourself and recognize the place where we are, then we can start rebuilding, building on a foundation, and do what we need to prepare for the terrain. We need to recognize what things need to go, what things need an overhaul, and what the new things are that we need to bring into our life. In the middle of that, only God can sustain us. It's like we are leaves on a tree – they are only green if the tree is healthy. We are the leaves and God is the tree.

There is one person that saw himself like a failure when he was young. And even though society saw him as a failure, his mom believed in him, and God believed in him. His name is Benjamin Carson (4) (Biography.com, 2019). Ben Carson was born in Detroit during a time when things were difficult for African Americans. The inner city of Detroit was the kind of place where somebody of Ben's age could end up in a gang or in prison. His mother forced him to go to the library almost every day, not knowing that she was laying the foundation. His mother, who was also a teacher, helped build the base by directing Ben in a self-discovery of his talents to run his race, to become the youngest director of a division of Johns Hopkins Hospital in Baltimore, director of pediatric neurosurgery, oncology, plastic surgery, and pediatric medicine. He became one of the best, if not the best, pediatric neurosurgeons in the world. He used his God-given talent to perform almost impossible surgeries on many children. He was the first one to perform a conjoined-twin separation at the age of 35. Dr. Carson didn't think he could run one mile, but God created him to run ultra-marathons, figuratively speaking. The point is that we all have talents given by God and we need to learn to see ourselves like a divine creation – one that is perfectly made. We have talents, but we will really win the race when we use our talents to help as many people as we possibly can.

Part of our inventory is to see what talents we have. Maybe we don't see them fully, but we can ask friends and family to tell us what they see in us. If our heart feels fulfilled when we are doing something for somebody or how we spend our time, then it must be because our talents are there. If we do something we like and it happens that we get paid for doing it, then we'll have success. Everything in this universe has a purpose, God created us in such way that we transform ourselves constantly, there is a purpose for each of our red blood cells, they last only less than half year, our body replaces itself about every 7 to 15 years, we get a full new skin every two to four weeks, our liver renews itself almost every two years, our brain changes, we can create, renew our mind, we can choose what we want to be, we can choose if we want to operate in the love zone, or in the fear zone. We are designed to love others and recognize the beauty in others.

Everything has a purpose and we have a purpose; we have a story and that is also part of our inventory. Everything in the universe has a purpose. Imagine that if everything has a purpose how it feels if you don't have one. Like somebody said, "Life is a process and your participation is required." You are unique and you are part of the world and what you do influence people around you, and what you do is a product of what you think. So, your mission, purpose in life, and your identity is your inventory.

Bon Appetit

So, I saw first where I was and then where I wanted to go. I saw my reality, and my change began with the foundation. That means we need to prepare for the terrain, we need to clear the field, and to clean the field. My friend from FIT, Marissa, had a normal life. But one day, everything changed for her. She discovered she had cancer. It was a sad surprise but made her think that anybody can have receive unexpected news. What you do you do when your best friend finds out they have cancer? Or you are told it might be just few years? Maybe you get scared, or maybe you start living those last days like you would never would. Maybe you learn to dance, maybe you learn to appreciate creation, maybe you will live to the maximum. Marissa went through three surgeries. Fortunately, she knew she had to start a new life filled with many changes and adjustments. This motivated her to start a healthy lifestyle. She had the need to clean her body and start building there. She felt, at that time, she had something toxic in her body and she needed to cleanse herself. The feeling was so strong it made her change her eating habits. She wanted to connect more with the natural and started throwing away unnatural processed foods. At the same time, she started engaging in sports. It was a time of many discoveries; anybody can motivate themselves when we put good things into our bodies. She started feeling better to the point that she decided to understand why she ate what she ate. She started to go deeper in the knowledge of the benefits of a good nutrition, and that the human being needs to be balanced, because at the end, in the same way we need balance in our life we need balance on our nutrition. We need carbohydrates, protein, fiber, good fats, we need balance in the emotional, social and spiritual areas or our life. I see it like a chair; if one of the legs brakes, the chair will fall, each leg is an area of our lives and we need each of them to be healthy. Life is a balance!

Veronica, like Marissa, also discovered that she needed new changes in her life. She starts her day with a breakfast with all the nutrients that she needs. It is different than what she used to eat because she has implemented new changes and habits in order to eat healthy. However, she thought the food she was taking was enough, but when she did her medical exams, she noted that she had a deficiency in certain nutrients, especially iron. This was in addition to her constant headaches and migraines. It felt like a vice grip was attached to her skull squeezing everything together. She understood that many ingredients found in superfoods are important. Now, Veronica drinks beet juice as if it's her daily coffee and she runs with amino acids on her belt to take one doses every five miles or so. Many of the ingredients that even runners take in packages sometimes are not the best choices. Her idea is to eat more organic plant-based foods with ingredients that are likely to be picked from a farm. Her smoothies are with spinach, kales, beets, and various fruits. Her proteins are from either animals or vegetables. She found it to be important to avoid red meats because they produce inflammation.

After she had her second child, Veronica started to exercise more regularly. But she experienced horrible migraines. Sometimes when she spoke about migraines, it seemed like nobody got it. It felt like it was a balloon inflating inside her head. The migraines limited her ability to accomplish her normal tasks, and running as well. It certainly affected her ability to be the best version of herself. But the right nutrition helped Veronica cope with the pain. She joined a small group of moms to start running, discovered the benefits of having her own space, and had the discipline to do something that gave her comfort and wellbeing. She experimented with these big changes. Before the birth of her son, she didn't have any regular routine, like many new mothers or people affected by their relationships. But she was able to adjust her time and use exercise not only as a way to be better, but as an exit from the mundane, day-to-day stress.

Marissa's studies gave her the possibility of choosing better and eating better. Even our meals need to be in balance. She understood how to combine meals, and created habits to get organized. She planned out what to eat during the day and for the week. Eating is not just getting filled with anything you can find; eating is nourishing our bodies. The way you eat is going to give you a better way of life. It will help you prevent sickness by improving your immune system. "I haven't been sick for the last three years," she said. She combines culturally not well-known foods, like spirulina, that are very nutritious superfoods. Marisa now is a nutritional health coach and has a certification in sports nutrition. She is in the process of discovering how to help other people while focusing on people who don't normally engage in sports activity. She wants to do a group that meets twice a week to walk, run a little bit, and connect with the natural.

The International Association of Athletics (5) (International Association of Athletics Federations, 2019) has recommendations for eating and drinking for health and performance, specifically designed for runners. A well-balanced diet can optimize training programs, maintain an ideal weight, reduce risk of injuries, and achieve high levels of performance. Food is our fuel and energy generator, sometimes we need to adjust the energy intake depending of the objectives. These objectives can be increasing muscle mass or reducing fat levels. The amount of energy available in our body is equal to the total dietary energy intake, minus the energy used for daily activity and training.

If the energy availability drops below a certain level, there might be substantial imparities of the metabolic and hormonal function. As a result, this can affect performance and health. If you are a sedentary person, the recommended intake of protein is 0.8 grams of protein per kg of body weight. But when you start to do heavy training, you need to increase the intake to about 1.2-1.7 grams of protein per kg of body weight. Proteins have been considered a key nutrient and energy generator for sporting success. This is attributed to the amino- acids makeup in proteins, as they are the building blocks for the production and repair of muscles. They aid in normalizing protein synthesis, assist with stabilization of muscle strength, endurance and volume and help to keep tissue firm. Lately, I have incorporated amino acids into my long runs in the form of a pill. I take one pill about every 5 miles. This combined with a drink of beet juice about 30 min before helps me keep my energy and helps with tissue maintenance. The amino acids that I take during the long runs are pre-digested 100% vegetarian protein and is comprised of non-soy legumes. As little as 10g of protein can have a good effect on endurance and resistance, with an optimal intake of 20-25 g. Good sources of protein are derived from animal like eggs, meats, fish, and poultry. They can also be found in certain vegetables, although it's important to consider the right intake as they are not as effective as animal sources.

Carbohydrates provide an important, but short, supply of fuel for exercise and they are stored in the form of glycogen. The targets for carbohydrate intake are about 1 g per kg of body weight per hour, consumed at frequent intervals for immediate recovery after depleting exercise. Between 0 to 4 hours, 3 to 5 g per kg of bodyweight per day for daily recovery from low volume training program, 5 to 7 g per kg of bodyweight for daily recovery from moderate training program, 6 to 10 g per kg bodyweight per day for recovery from moderate to heavy endurance training and carbo loading, and 10 to 12 g per kg bodyweight per day for maximized fueling for a distance event. These targets are recommended by the IAAF but can vary for different athletes. It is a good idea to visit a sport nutritionist that can provide expert advice.

Our Mind

I was at the airport in Indianapolis when an announcement on the speaker said that a woman left her "Unique Lipstick" at the security check point and needed to claim it. Can you believe that? I mean, people forget cell phones, tablets or even documents at security checkpoints, so I understand they need to go and get them. But an "Unique Lipstick"? Come on, if you bring a perfume or any liquid more than 100 ml you have to dump it. One day, they took my toothpaste because it was too big, but an "Unique Lipstick" must be really unique to make a person return for it. Well, I'll tell you what is unique – it's not the lipstick – it's the owner. She is so unique that she uses "Unique Lipstick". She is unique. I am unique. You are unique. In the 7.7 billion plus people on the planet, there is no one like you. Some people in the planet were created to help you and you were created to help some people in the planet. We all have at least one gift and one talent to serve others.

We won't understand others until we understand ourselves. We are uniquely brilliant; every thought comes from the depth of our identity, or I should say our identity comes from the depth of our thoughts and our mind. We all have a passion and we can benefit from our passion if we make it useful for somebody else, key word is useful. If we put the focus on ourselves all the time there is not success. If I become a servant of others then abundance will come. I can even build a business if I put my talents to give solutions to others. If I am generous with the world, the world will be generous with me. The main inventory in our lives is our mind, because our mind changes our brain, defines our identity and when we are clear of who we are we can accomplish the purpose for what we were created.

Dr. Caroline Leaf, a scientist that I admire greatly, talks about uniqueness in her book, The Perfect You (6) (Dr. Leaf, 2019). Maybe if your purpose is to touch many lives or just one live, it is the same, is your purpose. Maybe if your purpose is to leave a message in a book that is going to be read by millions of persons or maybe just for a handful of people, it doesn't matter, it is your purpose. In fact, even God has a purpose. The purpose of God is to love all people and to love you. You are so unique that if you were the only person in the world, God will love you to the point that if He would have to give His son only for you, He would do it. In fact, that is what He did. You need to understand who you are; low self-esteem happens when you don't understand who you are. Your mind is very powerful and can let you realize your purpose, or it can keep you from it. You can do things that look impossible or you can get paralyzed, it depends of what is in your mind. When we hear things that come to our brain, acoustic energy is interacting with the electromagnetic and quantum energy from the things we see and that energy is processed by our brain in thinking, feeling and choosing at 400 million actions per second. The brain has neurons that look like trees. These cells can look healthy, but toxic thoughts can deteriorate the neurons, causing these trees to dry. What we say and what we think, either healthy or toxic, will make healthy or unhealthy neurons. Chemical reactions happen and make growth the branches of the neurons, these branches uphold the memory, the brain can secrete passion and excitement chemicals, but stress or fear won't create chemicals, the brain will try compensate, will create excessive amount of the good chemicals, and will cause a chemical imbalance. The inflammation caused by this imbalance creates anxiety to the point that it can be paralyzing.

The mind is a powerful part of our being, it is the battle field where good ideas fight bad ideas. Am I going to stay on bed or I am going to get up and do something productive today? Am I choosing to be happy or am I not? Am I going to have a goal and work towards that goal or just simply let the time go by? We are product of what we put in our bodies. I am not talking only regarding the nutritional intake, but also what we put in our minds. What a person thinks, he is. How I am feeding my mind? Am I thinking whatever is noble, whatever is pure, whatever is true, whatever is admirable, whatever is excellent, whatever is edifying? Or am I just letting garbage and negative thoughts come into my mind? I heard the story about two dogs fighting. One was a good dog and the other a bad dog. Sometimes the bad dog was winning, sometimes the good dog was winning, and always the dog that was fed was the one that was winning. That is the kind of fight that takes place in our minds, depending of what kind of thoughts I decide to intake will determine which dog I am feeding. If I feed the mind with positive thoughts with faith then I'll become that way. I am transformed by the renewing of my mind. If you have toxic thoughts, you can create a bad reality, a soap opera, a "telenovela" in your mind. But this is not who you are, it is who you become. You can change that. The mind has the power to change your reality, you can unbecome who you have become, if for some reason you think negatively of yourself you can change that, you can be the best version of yourself. What you think can change your brain, which can change your intellect, your emotions, your behavior. This is going to manifest in everything you do, in business, in society, in the way you act, as a person, as a friend, as a mentor, as a runner, anything!

Dr. Caroline Leaf explains in her book "Who Switched off my Brain?" (7) (Dr. Leaf C., 2009), how healthy thoughts create healthy neurons and neuro connectors, and how toxic thoughts deteriorate our neurons. The Apostle Paul reminded us that we can be transformed by the renewing of our mind. Dr. Leaf teaches that the mind can change the brain, the mind is the command and the brain is the physical. If you have toxic thinking, this can affect your brain in a negative way but your mind has the power to change that. For example, perfect love casts out of fear. If I live in a realm of love, my thoughts, my emotions, and my actions will be aligned. But if I live in the realm of fear, there will be a negative impact in my thoughts, emotions and actions. 75 to 98% of current of mental, physical, emotional and behavioral illness come from our though life. Dr. Leaf has developed a system to detox our mind, to get rid of those toxic thoughts. Everything you say and do is first a though in your brain. Perhaps you can't change your circumstances, but you can choose to control your reactions to your circumstances by the thoughts that you put in your brain and by doing that, you are causing DNA to express and then you are storing a healthy though that in term will make your neurons healthy. Dr. Leaf illustrates this concept very well in her book. A healthy neuron literally looks like a tree with many radiant and healthy branches, a toxic neuron looks like a dry tree with few branches and is opaque. When you run a marathon and your body is telling you to go home and quit, and your mind is fighting it saying, "I can do this. I have followed my training plan for this. I came all the way here and I am going to cross the finish line." Then you are putting healthy thoughts in your brain and creating healthy neurons.

In a book called "SPARK!" (8) (Dr. Ratey, 2012), doctor John Ratey, MD. mentions that contrary to weight loss, the effects of exercise can improve the functions of the brain. It can boost your motivation, focus, and memory. Our brain can change, like the muscles change if they are exercised. Dr. Ratey talks about neuro connectors another term could be neurotransmitters. These are chemicals that run between neurons in our brain. The main chemicals are dopamine, norepinephrine, and serotonin. These three help us greatly in keeping us attentive, calm, and in general, in a state of wellbeing. Exercise helps to activate these neuro-connectors. Exercise can increase your ability to take on more information and retain it. Just 10 to 20 minutes of exercise in the morning can make you ready for the entire day. You will stay more alert, fresh, and feel well. This can be boosted if you do small seven minutes sessions two times a day. There is an app called the 7-min workout that shows you workouts that can be done at any time, and anywhere. Many times, people with moodiness, anxiety, and stress look for drugs, alcohol, or food to deal with their problems instead of exercising. This not only can reduce those problems, but it can also improve learning and memory. Find the time, at least 10 to 20 min a day, and it will make a huge difference. Use the stairs, park farther away, use the bike to go to the store, or walk to it. Do something!

No Fear

We cannot build up if we don't go overcome obstacles, whether it's laziness, the feeling of inadequacy, or fear. I have a friend who is a great pilot, artist and now swimmer. She has accomplished a lot since deciding to take on swimming. These are her thoughts, "Richard Bach once wrote, 'Argue for your limitations and sure enough, they're yours.' It's 25 meters to the other end. One year ago, I could not even make it halfway with my version of "swimming". Out of breath and exhausted in doing it wrong, I was afraid to put my head in the water. I wished to be a lap swimmer but I argued that overcoming the fear was impossible. I decided my 30+ year old fear had to go away. So, I took a few lessons on how to swim and got to work. It wasn't comfortable, but I didn't give up. Little by little I got my head down farther into the water. Finally, I could make one lap! Then after a few months, I swam three laps together as I found a rhythm. As spring arrived, I challenged myself to go ten laps, nonstop. Now, a year after giving up the argument, I'm up to 80 laps (a mile and a quarter) in my hour of swimming. I am a lap swimmer, and it is one of the most relaxing and rejuvenating activities in my life. Stop arguing for your limitations and start agreeing with your dreams." Ellen has found in swimming one of the most relaxing and rejuvenating activities of her life, but she couldn't build up on her laps if she didn't go head to head with her fear.

Some of the best years in my life were when I was missionary pilot in Albania; I learned so many things. When I first arrived to Albania, I had fear of the unknown. I didn't even know where Albania was located. I left Miami with $100 in my pocket to embark in one of the most wonderful adventures of my life, but I didn't really know anything about the country, the culture, or the language. Albania was living a tumultuous time. So, there I was, flying into Tirana, Albania, not even knowing the people that were going to pick me up at the airport. The only thing I knew was that God called me to that country to fly a helicopter with a Christian organization that uses the aircraft to bring hope to people in remote places. I joined a team to bring humanitarian aid, medical support, and words of encouragement to the suffering people of Albania. It was like going step-by-step not knowing what was ahead, but trusting fully in God. A few days later I was learning the language, telling everyone "Mier Dita", which means good morning in Albanian. Those who speak Spanish will get a crack out of this. By the third year, I had flown to more than 1,000 villages in the country by helicopter, taking teams to bring the word of God. We brought shoes to children that were walking in the snow with two rubber pieces of tires tied to their feet. We brought cloths, food, medicine, and doctors. We even brought a hospital bed to a person that couldn't move. I met the most incredible friends of my life there and left the country with a strong feeling of accomplishment. I was running my race. The fear was like a fog that wouldn't let me see ahead, I didn't know where the next turn was going to be. Sometimes we have a big goal, but we only see a few feet in the beginning, but that shouldn't stop us. We need to keep moving. Fear cannot paralyze us.

When I left Albania, it was in the middle of a civil war. An investing company came to the country and did a pyramid scheme; people were selling their homes, charging for one-years' worth of rent upfront, and taking their life savings to give it to this group that promised a very high return. When they lost their money, they panicked and blamed the government. They demanded answers and their money back. With no response, people's anger started to escalate into riots. Initially they broke into military and police outposts to steal arms. But later, the same police and military join the rebellious. CNN news showed images of Americans being air lifted from the American Embassy to navy ships on the Adriatic Sea. For me, it was time to take the helicopter out of the country to Italy. The flight was stressful because I had only enough fuel to cross the Adriatic Sea. I eventually landed in Bari with only a few minutes of reserve. I crossed the point of no return. The haze and fog were so thick that I had no visibility. Plus, I was only flying instruments, which is not the best situation in a helicopter. Suddenly, all my instruments started spinning and froze. I had to continue the flight with only reference to the speed indicator, the altimeter, and the compass. My GPS coverage was lost. It was terrifying to say the least, but I always felt God was with me. Sometimes we do things that we don't think we can do until the circumstances make us do it. Sometimes, people don't think they can run a marathon as they see it as something impossible. But when they take the first step at the start line, they know that they will finish the race. Sometimes we are in circumstances too difficult to bear and that there's no hope, but God will take us through it. We need to take a step of faith and we need to believe.

One time we were landing in Myrtle Beach; the day was beautiful. The skies were blue, yet there was an area of fog just over the airport a few miles around. When we landed at the airport, we were not able to see more that 1/4 mile because of the fog. The fog gave the impression that the whole city was covered and that everywhere else was the same. Sometimes you see things bigger than they really are. In reality, the fog that surrounded the airport could be contained in a gallon jar. We tend to make movies in our mind to make things seem more difficult than they really are. You'll think that you aren't going to make it, that 26.2 miles is too much, sickness is going to creep into your family, this job is too difficult. You need to just look at that fear and tell it, "You are just like a fog." Fear looks much bigger than it is. It looks more intimidating. Fear looks permanent but it's only temporary. Don't dwell on it because if you do, you will start imagining things and blow things out of proportion. You need to start moving. God will provide the light to see what's in front of you. Like driving in the fog, you have enough visibility to see only the road close to you, but little by little when you start moving forward, the next turn, the next mile will be revealed.

Habits

When I came back to running with Friends in Training (FIT), we ran one mile and we noted our time. This gave us the base for the training we are going to start. When the alarm sounded, it was still dark outside. All that my body was saying was that it didn't want to run that day. I woke up at 4:00 am and all I wanted to do was to roll over into my blankets and forget about everything. I wanted to forget that I made a commitment to run four times a week with a long run every Saturday. I wanted to forget that I started a plan to be followed. I think the hardest part of the training is getting your feet out of bed, sticking them on the ground, and getting up. Walking like a zombie, I made it to the bathroom and showered. Man, I thought, how crazy am I? Am I the only idiot getting up now to go running? But here we go, one more time, let's do this!

I drove 25 minutes on the expressway and got off on Sunrise Boulevard towards the beach. Only few cars were around me, I felt like a crazy guy going to run. What is that? I saw a car in front on me with a sticker with the numbers 26.2, I thought "He must be another crazy like me." I followed the car and surely, he drove to a parking lot where a bunch of people were getting ready to start running. I thought to myself, I am not the only one! That's great, I am going to enjoy this!

The first group that left was group B+ walkers – those running intervals of 1 minute and walking 1 minute. Nena is in this group. She is a sweet 72 years old lady that have been walking with FIT for more than 5 years. Walking can be a great exercise. Nena walked last year at the Keys 100; she did the 50 miles race, walking, and I can tell you that 49.9 of those miles were with a smile in her face. She started at 6:00 AM and finished around 11:00 PM. She was very tired, but had a smile. Nena just climbed the Kilimanjaro in Africa, another dream that came true for her. In most of her races, she wears T-shirts with a sign that says, "I am a walker." One day, I saw my friend Christina's baby taking his first steps and I told her, "Look at him, he is like Nena, he is a walker."

The second group was group B running intervals of 3 minutes and walking 1 minute. Then was the first group that I ran with, group C, running intervals of 5 minutes running and walking 1 minute. My coach was Maria Fletcher from England and my assistant coach was Anna Radushka from Russia. I remember having such love my first coaches because of their dedication. Following us was group D running intervals of 10 minutes running and 1-minute walking. And finally, group E running with no stops and a pace between 8:00 to 10:30 minutes per mile.

It takes time to build the base. Ben Carson made many trips to the library and read for days and days to be able to acquire the base knowledge needed to be propelled to the next level by his teacher. That became a habit. For a marathon the building of the base also takes time. A marathon training plan takes about 16 weeks. If you plan to race your first marathon, it's better to start early. Many experts recommend that people that want to run their first marathon run consistently a base mileage for at least a year before doing a full marathon training program. Sometimes we want to do things too fast, we want instant results, we live in a microwave culture. If We are patient and faithful in the little, God will bring bigger things because we will be faithful in the much. Is better to start with small races like 5Ks, 10Ks, and eventually a half marathon. The key is consistent running of about 20 to 30 miles per week. If we try to build miles too quick, too soon, we might find ourselves with an injury. Easy running is the base of your running. It is like the foundation of a house, when you have built the capacity to run for long distance, you can build on it.

Easy running can help you to strengthen your cardiovascular system, you'll get a stronger heart. The speed to develop the base is a speed when you can have a normal conversation effortless, it is called conversational pace. I remember when I started running with FIT, I saw people talking while running while I was puffing and puffing. I was silent because my breathing wouldn't allow me to talk, but that changed with time. You can do different types of workouts to build your easy running. One of those is a long, slow run once a week or a recovery run after a hard workout. You can also do a steady-state run, which is a little bit faster than conversation-pace. Or you can do a progressive long run, where you can run faster and faster as the miles increase. You can also do a long-tempo run where you can run faster for the first part of the training, followed by conversation-pace run, and finished by a faster pace as the beginning.

If you are a beginner marathon runner you should build from the 20 to 30 miles per week and eventually aim to build a weekly mileage up to 40 or more miles. This will take time, so you should start doing it at least four months before the race day. This can be accomplished with three to five runs per week. In my case, I run speed training on Tuesdays, tempo-run on Thursdays, long-run on Saturdays, and another easy run on Sundays. These runs should be mostly in a conversation pace. The speed training and tempo is where you can stretch up, but it's convenient to take breaks. When building base mileage, never increase your weekly mileage by more than 10 percent from week to week.

It took patience to rebuild my spiritual life. I created habits, which also meant discipline. Discipline is a word that is not fun, but my motivation was so high that I had to do it. I knew that could be only be done with discipline, and I think discipline starts with habits. Like the farmer that starts preparing his crop, I put my hand on the plow and I haven't looked back. We need to start at the foundation. The terrain needs to be prepared, and for me, this means I would need to be clean. I knew I couldn't do it by myself. If I try to clean my spirit by myself, I am always going to fall short. I will never be able to cross the finish line. Yet, Jesus did that for me. His blood can clean us whiter than snow. My reality changed in a moment. Now, I am not a failure. I am "under construction". I can build a new me, but there is a price to be pay, but Jesus did so for us. Now, I can cross the finish line. It is the same as my running. We need to start with a base. I am going to build my house on the rock. Winds and storms will come, but I will be able to stand if I build my house on that rock, and for me, that rock is Jesus. Once I have cleaned the terrain, found the rock to build on, I need to use the right materials to support the house. For my running, that means to have an aerobic base, a pace where you can run with a heart rate that can maintain the body for many miles. For my body, this means eating the right nutrients. For my business, this means finding my vision and the mission. For my soul, this means to forgive and ask forgiveness. I needed to forgive all those that have hurt me and I needed to forgive myself! Things are not always the way I wanted them to be, but God always gives us a second chance. We will get up, we will run our race, and we will cross the finish line!

My foundation is to surrender my life to Christ and to live in his presence. He calls it "Abiding in Him". I am connected to the source of my energy, and from there, I can start building. Actually, the surrender is daily and influences the way I live day-by-day. I decided to live in the present moment. I am going to enjoy every single moment that the day brings me. Once I get out of bed every morning, I put my feet on the floor and I say to myself, "This is where I am right now, in this place and time. I am not in my past. As soon I take the first step, I am living this day." There is a quote that says, "Yesterday is history, tomorrow is a mystery, today is a gift, which is why we call it the present."

Yokoi Kenji, a Colombian motivational speaker with Japanese parents, tells a story of one of his teachers. It says life is like that guy, that guy that is trying to escape from the tiger, and the tiger is almost catching up to him to eat him. He is approaching a cliff and makes the decision to jump. He falls down the cliff but reaches to grab a branch from a tree that is hanging out. He spends the night hanging from the tree with the hope that the next day he could fall and the bottom isn't so far down. The next day, he wakes up and the sun shines on a berry that he couldn't see the night before. The first thing he sees looking down is the tiger, waiting for him to come down. He looks at the berry again. The berry is ready to eat. As he places the berry in his mouth, it breaks open with a rich flavor that quenches his thirst. And that's the end. "Wait a minute," Yokoi asked, "Where is the tiger, what happen to the tiger?" The teacher said, "The tiger doesn't matter, the berry is the important thing." What? And the tiger? the teacher continued the class, and Yokoi, raised his hand one more time and asked, "And the tiger? What happened with the tiger?" He asked so much that the teacher said, "The tiger doesn't matter, stop asking about the tiger."

The tiger means death and death sooner or later is going to come to us and get us. But the berry, the berry is that small thing in life that nobody can take away. That is why we need to enjoy the berry to the fullest. Sometimes we don't enjoy the berries because we keep thinking about the tiger. We don't enjoy Monday, Tuesday, Wednesday because we keep thinking about the weekend. We don't enjoy January, February, March because we keep thinking about summer vacation. We don't enjoy the 5, 8, 10 miles run because we're thinking about the great marathon. We don't enjoy the rain, the dark, the solitude because all we want is the sunshine and the company. Let's enjoy the berries. Let's put the berries in our months until our lips are tinted with red. Let's taste the flavor and feel the texture in our mouths. Let's enjoy the small things in life, every day and every moment. Let's live the in the present and to the fullest. As I am writing this, I am flying over Cuba. The beautiful blue sky is shining over a carpet of cotton-like white clouds. To the West, a line of clouds cut the bright orange sun that is setting on the horizon. To the East, a big, white, full moon. The sight is gorgeous and I am going to enjoy this. I am going to taste my berry.

Living in the present means that we need to start focusing little-by-little on the things that will shape us, those building blocks are the good habits that we implement in our lives. First, we shape our habits and then our habits shape us. To build the base, we need to select the best building materials. We need the consistency that good habits can give us. Our brains like repetition and likes to go into autopilot with the minimum effort. Our brains like to stay in the routine that we have. That is why we need to bring new routines that our brain can repeat, but will take our life to the places we want to go. We can get to a point where our daily habits can take decisions for us instead of us taking decisions based on the emotions that we are experiencing. To create habits, we need to start with the right thoughts. These thoughts bring emotions. Emotions bring actions and consistent actions create habits. My new habits include starting and finishing my day by giving thanks, for the good and the not so good. I start my day with prayer, meditating on what the Lord says to me, and writing about what I am learning in a journal. Good habits are difficult to form but will help us to live easier and better. Bad habits are easy to form, but will give us a hard life. The bad habits that we have are rooted in our brains and the only way to leave them is by replacing them with good ones. We become what we think, that is our vision, we need to write our goals, meditate on them, and act upon them. The hardest part is to get started. Last year I ran almost 1,700 miles and completed the challenge of running 1,000 miles in one year with the encouragement of a running club called "1,000 miles Run Club". Their motto says, "A Journey of a Thousand Miles Begins with One Step". So, take action on your new habits! One step at a time. A Thousand Miles Begins with One Step.

Our life depends greatly of what we do every day. We take for granted the small things that we do daily, but if we apply the compound effect to our day, we'll see great results. Maybe a 15-minute run isn't much, but if we read every day for 15 minutes, it will make a great difference. Maybe $5 isn't much, but if we save $5 every day, we can have a large amount of money after a number of years if we apply the compound effect. Fifteen minutes of exercise everyday can shape our bodies, but this need to be constant habit.

The habits that Marissa developed were followed in such a way that now she can't go back. It gives her too much satisfaction to live the way she does now. She doesn't want to eat anything bad and she doesn't have to be on any special diet, she just has a new lifestyle. These are habits that don't happen in one week, it takes time, patience and work. And then you don't want to change it for anything. This means discipline. In the case of sports, Marissa had the need to energize her body and decided to run. For her, running means to always move forward without stopping. This gives her strength, security, and it's also a time that she has for herself to think and a way for her brain to get oxygen. When she runs, she thinks about the good that she gets from running. She feels so good that she wants more.

When I talked about habits with my coach Luis, he mentioned that we all have habits. Good habits can make a person prosperous and healthy, and bad habits make a person poor or sick. Those habits can make your days shorter, or can add years. We are not born with habits; we build our habits. Habits are like a key; the bad habits open doors to things that are not worthy, that are not beneficial. The good habits open doors to good things and to blessings. My question for you is, what door are you opening? Are you opening the door to unhealthy things that are going to deteriorate your body and your mind? The key is in your hands because you are the one that has to build the habit and use it. There are social, health, professional, and spiritual habits – all of which are important and related. For example, I believe spiritual habits connect the spiritual realm with the physical realm. If I am in peace with God and if I abide in Him, that is going to be manifested in the natural. When I am running, I have a special time to enjoy God's company and God's creation. I see how a healthy habit can be connected to a spiritual habit. Identify good habits, change your old habits, reevaluate what habits you have, and leave those that are not healthy. It takes 28 days to create habit and 60 days to reinforce it. Once you acquire a habit, it will relieve your brain from making decisions.

To make adjustments and to create a training plan, we need to begin with the end on mind. For the Berlin Marathon, my goal was to finish between 4:00 and 4:15; this would mean that my pace needed to be in average 9:00 to 9:10 minutes per mile. With this information, my coach, Luis Aguilar, was kind enough to build a training plan for me. This plan will show exactly day by day during the 16 weeks of preparation how long and how fast I needed to run and what kind of running I should be doing during the week. If I have a goal on mind I can go backwards and start working on my little goals. My goal in life could be to have a business that will grow to become a successful enterprise. It could be to become financially independent. Or it could be to run the six major marathons in Berlin, London, Tokyo, New York, Chicago, Boston. It could simply be to run one marathon in my life, or to run one marathon a year. Perhaps to finish my career as a successful engineer, or to become a doctor, or have the best restaurant. Whatever the goal is, if we begin with the end in mind, we can start with the base and work our way up with small goals, yearly goals, monthly goals, and daily goals. These will bring us closer to the end. As we achieve our goals, we can create habits that help. We can overcome an old mindset and renew it. The reward is not in the results; the reward is in doing it. And if we have good habits, we can do it better.

I have another habit to run three to four days a week, speed training on Tuesdays, easy run on Wednesdays with my friends from We Run Weston. I have Fartlek on Thursdays, which is a Swedish word that means "speed play" and is a combination of continuous training with interval training. In other words, fast running mixed with slow running. Then I have a distance run on Saturdays with my friends from FIT, Long Runs and Fumigaos. When running a marathon, especially at the end, some people can't keep going with the same energy. It's like their fuel tank is empty. They hit the wall, then they are "Fumigao" – a Spanish term that means "dead". They essentially fall like a fly by not following their plan and training.

Other habits that I developed are when I turned my traveling times in a car into a university. I have spent hours of training, listening to investing, real estate, personal development, spiritual life, Christian teachings, credit repair, entrepreneurship, and healthy-related talks. I started having a journal and reading books, morning devotionals. I cut out the TV and only watch audiovisual content. It is necessary create habits to give the brain a routine and get used to repetitions that are going to bring us to a better place.

Another good habit is to celebrate. Celebrate the small accomplishments and the big milestones. When I complete a sale, I celebrate, even if it is just taking my kids for ice cream. It was a beautiful day with a glorious sunrise, we completed our first 10 miles, we were heading back to the park and the coaches and runners of FIT were waiting for us. They had a finish line with a ribbon surrounded by balloons and with Hawaiian music in the background. As we crossed the finish line, we were received with a Hawaiian lei and a celebration. It was the celebration for our first ten miles. Don't let go of those moments, your kid's good grades, birthdays, goals accomplished, always make a point to celebrate.

One habit that helped motivate me is my morning power hour. I have put my dreams and goals in a presentation with pictures. It's a compilation of my dreams, and in seeing them every day, I visualize them as if I already have them. For example, I want to be a better dad. So, I have a picture of my children and

I visualize myself like being the greatest dad. I want to be the greatest pilot, so I visualize myself as that. I want to qualify for the Boston marathon, so I have a picture of the finish line of the Boston Marathon and a date next to it. That is my visualization time. Everything that happens in the realm of what you can see, happened before in the realm of what you can't see. That is faith – seeing yourself as who you are, where you want to be, what you want to do, and what you want to have. I start my morning power hour by drinking two glasses of water with lemon, meditating with God, and writing my affirmations. I write for few minutes of how I am and how God sees me. I declare on paper that I am all those wonderful things that I have on the list. Then I do my visualizations. Then, I'll exercise by doing pushups and sit-ups. Finally, I read for something for ten minutes that lifts me up, all the while sipping on a great Columbian coffee.

In summary, to build the foundation, there are three key factors to consider: consistency, strength, and habits. Most of the marathon training programs are 16 weeks, but even before you jump in your first plan, you need to do a pre-marathon preparation. To be consistent as runners, we slowly add distance to our runs. Also, we need to consistently do a number of runs per week. This can be three or four times a week, or even more for those who are more advanced and have more challenging goals. For beginners, three times a week is okay. But the important thing is to build a schedule and stick to it. The idea is to get use to running consistently, and focusing on posture and technique. At this point, there is no need to pay attention to running longer or faster; you just need to create the habit of running certain days of the week.

The base is the capacity to run a certain number of miles in a comfortable way; this will dictate the intensity of the training. You get to be FIT in the physical, but a mental FIT and a soul FIT is equally important in running a good race. If you keep in mind why are you running, whether it's to accomplish a goal or a dream, it will give you the drive to endure the training and to face the difficulties during the race. In life, it's important to keep in mind your WHY – what inspire you. What is your purpose and what is your passion? Mark Allen (9) (Phillips, 2019), a six-time Hawaiian Ironman champion, talks about to find a quiet place in everything you do, developing mental toughness. In a race, for example, if the little voice inside you is telling you that you are not going to make it, things start getting out of shape in your mind. Then, you need to breath deep, and get to that quite place to put you in the right frame of mind. You may want to start before the race or training to first find that quiet place, then translate that sensation when you are in motion (Phillips, 2019). I talked previously about making new habits. For me, a new habit that I developed is to start the day in a quiet place, giving thanks, and meditating in the goodness of God and praying to Him. This sensation can be transferred to the race. When your mind starts going in the direction of quitting, feeling pain, or disqualifying yourself, you can come to that quiet place. Then, start bringing in new, positive, and strong thoughts. Get to a point when you relax, listen to your breath, look around and say this is life, and this is great. This is renewing your mind and is living in the present. I am living this moment now. I am enjoying this berry.

There are a million of reasons why you can't. Find the reason why you CAN and you are golden. Find your WHY, and don't let it go.

Ana Maria Villegas

Photo by: Ana Maria Villegas

Photo by Luis Tovar

It doesn't matter how fast or how far. It doesn't matter if today is your first day or if you've been running for twenty years. There is not test to pass, no license to earn, not membership card to get. You just run.

Friends in Training

Photo by Luis Tovar

We have our own race but we can run it together.

Chapter 2.
BUILD UP

Preparation

You have your base stablished. You feel comfortable running 10 to 15 miles. Now is time to think about the race that is coming. Now is when you can build on your base. You need to prepare for the Marathon that is ahead. Preparation is crucial, but you need to prepare for success also. If I prepare for something, then I am taking that task seriously. I prepare for the day, a meeting, a class, or for a job. In anything we do, preparation is the key for success. If I am not successful in certain areas of my life, maybe it's because I am not well prepared. For a field to yield crops, there needs to be preparation. The land needs to be cleared, the soil needs to be plowed, the seed needs to be planted, and it needs to be watered. Only after the right preparation will the fruit come. My life is a field that is constantly in preparation. The fruit is given by the Spirit of God and that is love, joy, peace, patience, kindness, goodness, faithfulness, gentleness, and self-control. The preparation is prayer, faith, believing, living in a relationship with God, and allowing Him to come and prepare the crop. In everything you do, prepare yourself and ask, what can I do to make myself ready? If you want to finish the race successfully, you need to prepared for it.

Miami and South Beach are two of the world's most popular vacation spots. They are vibrant places with people from all over the world. My running buddies are from Argentina, Bolivia, Brazil, Colombia, Costa Rica, Korea, Russia, India, Jamaica, Venezuela, UK, Israel, and all over USA, you name it. South Florida is a place of contrast and one of the only places I've seen Russians dancing salsa. You can find high-end Latin cuisine and traditional home cooking. South Florida is home to the key lime pie and the tequeños, the espresso and the cortadito. You have the bustle of Calle Ocho and the historic hideaways of Coral Gables. It is one of the few places where people speak Spanglish. I hate when radio hosts talk in Spanglish, "Oye mija, puse el pollo in the oven, and I hope no se me queme, epale niña vamos a janguear en la marketa." That's the people of South Florida. But the best thing about South Florida is the people and the Miami Marathon!

The Miami Marathon requires a lot preparation. The marathon of 2017 was a special one because it was celebrating 15 years. Just few weeks before the marathon, the director came to Friends in Training to promote the race. It was a special moment because our leader Marcela has ran every single Miami Marathon. She bought T-shirts from every single marathon; I don't think anybody has such a collection. At the expo, more than 24,000 people come from all over the world to pick up their packages. The weather was beautiful with a clear sky. But the next day was a contrast; it was a rainy, cold, overcast, and windy day. After many weeks of preparation, I could say that I really have built up my capacity and was really excited to make a personal record. Many people came to the race with ponchos or plastic garbage bags to protect their upper bodies from the rain. I opted for the garbage bag, and it really helped. My strategy was to run the whole race doing a Galloway schedule. We followed the schedule with my friends Ana Maria and Marisa, although Ana Maria was only going to be with us for the first half. The idea was to run for one mile, walk for one minute at a pace of 15 minutes per mile, and a 10:30 min per mile during the run. We were synchronized, running like a Swiss watch. But when Ana Maria left because she was doing only half, suddenly all the music and the cheer stopped and it got really quiet. We kept the pace with Marissa, but unfortunately, she had a cramp at mile 23. So, she stayed a little bit behind, and even though it was cold, everyone's cheers kept us warm.

This is why we make our hearts stronger and we eat better. But to run the distance, we need to strength our muscles. There are few exercises that help us build resistance. Our habits should include time to exercise. Our muscles give stability to our bones and provide balance. We not only need to exercise them, but stretch and warm them. Few exercises help us strengthen our abdominals, knees, gluteus, hamstrings, quads, and calves. Exercises like single leg deadlifts, single leg mini squats, curtsy lunges, walking lunges, squats, planks, side planks, among others, can develop the strength we need to run faster and longer. Whether you chose to do it at the gym, at home or outside, let it become a habit. Running three days a week and doing two days of strength exercises is a good plan. Focus on working the areas you need to. I do two sets of 15 repetitions each, twice a week, whatever your number is, follow through. Make it happen. Don't give 99.9%, give 100%. The better the workout, the better the results. We are aiming for quality. Exercise can help with the function of the knees, increase aerobic capacity, muscle strength, reduce mortality by 27%, and reduce cardiac mortality by 31%. It also improves physical function, quality of life, reduce depression, hypertension, and control or prevent diabetes to name a few.

Strength exercises help diminish the loss of muscle tissue with the aging process. For maintaining good running form, strengthening the core muscles is very important. This will help stabilize the hips and knees and prevent injuries. When one muscle group is weak and not efficient, the body will try to compensate with other muscles. This in turn creates an imbalance between opposite muscle groups. When the muscles are strong, they maintain the alignment of the joints, eliminating or minimizing the imbalance. Our leg muscles are trained mainly for endurance, not for strength, so strength training can help you to generate force.

If your muscles can't gain strength, they will take more work. Some exercises can help your body perform better in a full range of motion, like squats and lunges. Balance can be improved with exercises like single-leg mini squats or single-leg deadlifts. Example of core exercises are different forms of planks. Muscle strength can be obtained with exercises that work specific muscles of the body, like calves, hamstrings or gluteus. These muscles are important because they support and bring stability to the whole body during those full range motions. Running can only get you up to certain point. You will need to do activities other than running. It's very important to add some cross training to your week with biking, swimming, or going to the gym. You can even do workouts using your body weight at home or in the park. It is important to calendar at least two days a week for strength training. For me, Wednesdays and Fridays are my days of strength training. Finally, one of the most important aspects of the preparation is daily mobility and movement sessions; they need to be a habit. In some spare time of every day, dedicate ten or fifteen minutes to taking care of your body. You can do couch stretches, foam rolling stretches, calf rolling, or foot rolling. Last Saturday, I was running 20 miles and I felt a little discomfort on my right quadriceps and I knew that I needed to attack this area with strength training.

We are made to run. Our bodies are built for long distance running; a study called the "Science of Marathon Running" (10) (PBS Digital Studios, 2016) elaborates on this. Humans compete with many animals and beat them through long distance running. The Cheetah, for example, can run only about two miles before overheating. The adaptation for long distance running of the human body was key for hunting activities in the early world. We have enlarged ear canals that help us balance while we are running. Considering we make contact with the ground with only one foot 100% of the time, this is the importance of balance exercises. Our eye reflexes help us to maintain our brains with no motion as we move up and down. Short arms and thin ankles help us not make so much effort when we swim. Wide shoulders, a thin waist, and narrow pelvis help us counter the rotation when we are moving our legs. Sweat glands, less body hair, and thin bodies helps us cold down by dispersing heat very quickly. The blood flow from the brain can keep it cool. Big gluteus maximus muscles help you stabilize the upper body. High surface area joints in hips, knees, and ankles help for shock absorption. The lower muscles of the legs are built like rubber bands; every time our body hits the ground, it delivers up to eight times the force of our body. It is like 1,400 lbs. hitting the floor, and this force lands on a very small surface of our foot. God created in us a lever system that dissipates this force as the force go upwards to reach the brain with zero impact. Our feet expand and spread like a shock absorber. The Achilles' tendon, allows flexibility in the calf's muscles, and the ankle to act a as a lever to absorb up to 50% of the energy. By using stored kinetic energy instead of chemical energy, we can go farther with less work.

The power for running is delivered in form of ATP (Adenosine Triphosphate). This is produced by our muscles through two proteins, actin and myosin. Muscle contraction is produced by the myosin heads. The active site of actin is exposed to Ca^{2+} binds troponin, the myosin head forms a cross-bridge with actin. During the power stroke the myosin head bends, ADP plus phosphate is released, a new molecule of ATP attaches to the myosin head, causing the cross-bridge to detach. ATP hydrolyzes to ADP and phosphate which returns the myosin to the initial cocked position to start a new contraction. Our muscles have only a couple seconds of ATP stored, so we are constantly replenishing it. A body that weighs about 165 lbs. recycles about 75 kg of ATP during a marathon, almost the entire body weight. This 75 kg of ATP releases the same amount of energy as a kilogram of TNT in an explosion. Our body gets ATP in a couple of ways; if we run full speed at an anaerobic pace, our cells will use an inefficient process called Glycolysis. By running at a slower pace, our body will use a better process called the Krebs Cycle and the Electron Transport Chain. By using glycolysis, our body produces about 2 units of ATP per glucose. By using the Krebs cycle, our body produces about 38 units of ATP per glucose. Our body will require more glucose to produce ATP at full speed, and the energy will be obtained from sugar. At a slower pace, a lesser amount of glucose is required to produce more ATP, as the energy is taken from fat. This is another important factor for nutrition before and during the race, to produce the glucose and glycogen for the race.

To think of all the many functions that our body accomplishes while long distance running makes me in awe of our creator. The human body is the most amazing machine. When a doctor saw how perfect our body was, he went from being an atheist to a believer in God. At the age of 15, one of his best friends with his family were victims of a murder. He taught himself that God shouldn't allow this to happen. He ran away from God. He got angry with God and became an atheist until he studied the human body. He couldn't fathom how the human body was so perfect. He thought it was a piece of art and that something with that order could come from disorder. The only thing he could think is that an artist, a creator, was the reason for the human body to be. The doctor explains that physics says that unless there is an outside force, order moves to disorder. This is a conflict with the biological idea that everything is a form of evolution. In this conflict, he surrendered his life to God. Our body can respond to the demand of a race and our mind can tell our body what to do, and how to do it.

Form

When I came to the US, I felt I was less than others. Like many immigrants that started again in this country, I had to do random jobs. I delivered newspapers in New York with my cousins. We had to work long hours at night carrying piles of newspapers and then tossing them along a route to dozens of houses. The hardest part of the job was to do it in Winter because we had to drive with the windows open. Not to mention the conditions of the roads after snow fall were challenging to drive. I remember one night when we had to go up a hill and the roads where covered with freezing rain. One lady that worked in a deli shop was waiting at the top of the hill to go to work and was afraid of going by herself. She asked us if we could give her a ride to the bottom of the hill to the deli shop. She told us that if we take her down, she would give us a bagel with coffee. We start heading down and the only way to get some traction was to go downhill with the gear in reverse. It was a big challenge to get down, but we made it. That was the best bagel and coffee that I have ever eaten.

After almost two years of delivering newspapers and learning English, I came to Florida and I worked as a construction handy man, and later as a taxi driver. I don't have anything against these jobs because all work that is ethical and decent is honorable. On the contrary, I have deep respect for people that do any job entailing hard labor. But it was hard on my ego; I was a military pilot and was used to doing other types of work. I remember one time when I picked up two pilots from the airport to bring them to the hotel. They looked neat in their uniforms. When I looked one of them closely from the mirror, I realized it was one of my classmates in the Air Force academy. I felt happy for him that he was flying for a prestigious airline. But at the same time, I felt sorry for myself because I barely made enough to make ends meet. I used to walk with my head low, my back vent forward, and not paying attention to the form. Now when I look back, I know that God was teaching me two things: the first one is that a persons' identity is not in their career, but in who they are, and second, that I am perfectly made. I am created in the image of God, my citizenship is in heaven, I am a prince of the King of Kings, Lord of Lords, and that I belong to God. This changed the way I looked at myself. It changed my form. I don't walk with my head low anymore; I walk with my head high. I am proud of myself because my Heavenly Father is proud of me. I know this because I am proud of my children. I walk like a prince, like an ambassador, like a son of a King, and that is because it is who I am. You are also beautifully made in the image of God; you are like the pupil of His eye. Even if you are going through difficult times right now, you can walk with your head high and with form because God is proud of you.

I learned a lot about form from my friend Christina. She started her experience in running when she went to work for a running store in Miami. She learned a lot about running during her time there from runners and from the owners whom treated her like a daughter. She learned from different people that came to the store with different injuries, how a shoe can be good for one person but not good for another person. But the most important thing she learned about was form. Sometimes I notice that some of my friends at the last part of long runs are looking down, their backs bent forward, and arms just hanging. They don't pay attention to their form.

Christina teaches FIT members about form. She made videos of everyone in the class and analyzed them to show areas that need to be corrected. Posture and form are how you place or move the parts of your body for proper running. These are some recommendations for a good running posture:

- Shoulder blades: You want to have a slight retraction of your shoulders. This means your shoulder blades need to be slightly back. This will help with lung expansion and better capacity for breathing.
- Head position: Your head needs to be straight, looking forward. Your chin should not be forward and not looking down. This will help keep your airways clear for better breath circulation.
- Arms position: Some people run with their arms too far from the body, or the arms and hands all over the place. The arms should be slightly touching your rib cage and shouldn't be crossed in front of your chest. Your arms should be in a 90-degree angle.
- Core: You need to activate your core, but avoid excessive rotation of your core. The activation can help you with your hip positioning for a more efficient run.
- Feet positioning: Avoid internal or external rotation of your feet. Think of how you are going to land. You need to land on your mid-foot.

Now putting all of this together, you need to have a slightly forward lean in your body. One time I had a hip pain and I realized that this happened because I was running with my upper body straight up, almost with a very slight backward lean. If you run very straight, gravity's force will go down straight to your heels, causing pressure in your hip.

Form is directly connected to range of motion or flexibility. Good form requires good flexibility. For this reason, a key element in staying flexible is stretching. Also, when running, it is important to stay relaxed because muscle tension can reduce running economy. If we keep a mental check of our form and be relaxed, we will be more efficient. Avoid exaggerated knee lifting and over-striding. Try not to land too far beyond your center of gravity.

Basically, there are three running foot strikes. Nate Helming (11) (Holly, 2017), of The Run Experience, explains very well how to have a proper foot strike and how to improve it.

- Heel style strike: This is when the heel hits the ground first.
- Mid-foot strike: When the whole foot hits the ground at the same time, but mainly the mid-part of the foot.
- Forefoot-style strike: When the forward part of the foot hits first. Some people say that the heel strike is bad, but really there are times when we use any of these strikes.

In general, mid-foot strike is the best. What is bad is when we use the wrong strike for the wrong situation for extended periods of time. Many people with a cadence problem use the heel strike for long slow runs and this is bad. This might be due to stiff hips, poor core strength, and lack of arm swinging. If I go down on a steep hill and I need to put the brakes on, that's when I use the heel strike. But as soon as I am on a flat surface, I should go back to mid foot strike. If I want to spring to the finish line, a front-foot strike is the best, but if used for long periods of time might be hard on your toes. I have seen people that have developed blisters, and even losing toenails, on a marathon due to the excessive use of the front foot strike.

For Christina, running was like a therapy. She competed for few years in triathlons and half marathons. She learned by herself about training methods. The times when she was running alone were special times for her because she meditated. She felt like she was connecting with herself and with God. At the time, she felt confused about who she was, and maybe she didn't imagine that God would use her to help people like me. If I think about form, it's because of what Christina taught me. When we hit the bottom, there is no other way to go but going up, and that is what happen to Christina and running was a big help in her new journey. Running gave her opportunities to reflect, clean her thoughts, get rid of what was bad, and embrace what is good. It was a time to get in a better form.

I Need You

Even if you are going through very difficult times, God is with you. You are not alone. Believe it or not, there is a difference when you train by yourself and when you train with a group. When you run alone, it's like you're in a bubble. You feel every step and every mile like you are by yourself; there is nothing wrong with that. But when you put the dynamics of a group, or another person, into the mix, it is different. You don't feel alone. You're next to somebody who understands you and feels the same way you are feeling. It's not a burden since you look forward to seeing your friends. You laugh together, you cry together, and support each other. You are like buddies, and this can help you. It is what Friends in Training can give you. We are all in training, but we are friends.

During the Berlin Marathon, I had a cramp in my soleus muscle that made me limp almost half of the race. When I came back home, I needed help figuring out how to get better. I am so thankful for the angel that God sent to me, Christina. I realized it took a cramp to reach out to her, but God used that pain to bring me something better. Christina gave me a routine of exercises for muscle strength that I follow three times per week and have passed to other friends. That is how God works: You have a need, you realize that you have to reach out to somebody, and that you can't do everything by yourself. God provides the help that you need through other people. You get the benefit, and then pass it on to other people. If you take all that God has given you and keep it for yourself, you are cutting off the blessing for somebody else. That is the main reason I am writing this book, except for the fact that I felt compelled by God to write the message that He gave me. I want to share what has worked for me, and what I have learned from other professionals and from other runners, in the physical and the spiritual. I respect what is working for you, but still I want to pass on my blessing. It is like the song by Reba McEntire (12) (Roth, 1983) that goes like this:

A smile is not a smile until wrinkles your face

A bell's not a bell without ringing

A home's not a home when there's nobody there

A song's not a song without singing

AND LOVE ISN'T LOVE 'TILL YOU GIVE IT AWAY.

If you have something to offer, give it away, and if you need something, reach out and ask for help

Heather Dornidem was a track runner competing for the university of Minnesota. She was running the finals in the women's 600-meter dash in 2008. In her final lap, she was in the lead when her feet tangled with another runner and she fell. When she got up, she was already behind all the runners. In this race, it felt almost too short to catch up. But she got up and start catching up to the third place, then second. Everybody knew that she was running faster than anybody else and it was a matter of having enough track to take over the first runner. She did it – she overtook the first runner and ended winning the race by 0.04 seconds. She fell, but still she won. Many remember this unbelievable race because she never gave up. In an interview, Heather mentioned that what made her come back that strong was helping the team, and the idea that yes, she can do this. If we fall in life, that doesn't mean that we lose our race. Yes, we can get up, and yes, we can win, and yes, we can do this.

Life may not always go the way you want, but you can still win. I see the story of many of my friends from Venezuela that had a turn in their life, but they are still winners. Some of them are doctors that had to drive a taxi, engineers that had to wash floors, and architects that had to wait tables. They had a fall in their lives but they got up and found better jobs where they learned to honor those who are selling flowers on the street or answering phones in a call center. They discovered that anybody that does an honorable job is an honorable person. They know that your identity is not related to what you do, but it is who you are.

When you have an unexpected turn in your race, it is hard to believe that you are going to win. God doesn't believe this way. He knows what it is to fall; it happened to him when he was carrying his own cross. But he got up and went to victory. So, I am writing to you, my champion friend. If you are blessed, happy, and fulfilled, good for you. Enjoy it and be thankful. But if you had fallen and feel like the race is too hard to survive, I am telling you like Heather's race, don't give up. God will never give up on you. He has given you the victory. You are a winner.

So, we talked about the base and once we have the base it's time to build up. Before adventuring to run a marathon, it's better to start with smaller races, 5k, 10k, half marathon, each has its own training plan and if we are patience we will get there, progressively you will need to build time and distance. First things first, get ready to run shorter distances. Make that a part of your routine. I live in Weston, Florida, and we have a very nice group that runs on Wednesdays. The group is sponsored by Baptist Health System and is a way to bring healthy options to the community. The Baptist Weston Run Club is very fun and I have met some of my best friends there. We usually meet on Wednesday nights and run for about 4 miles at any pace you want. I encourage you to find a small group to run short distances and go for it. If you consider yourself to be in not very good shape, or if you are not used to running, you can start run-walking until you are able to run about 30 minutes nonstop. By that time, you should be ready for a 5K. Then, you can start training for a 10k. Once you can run for about 60 minutes nonstop you should be ready for a 10k. Then you can start a 12 to 14 weeks training program for a half marathon incorporating the tempo runs, Fartlek, and speed training in your routine. FIT is a group that helps people to reach this goal, the main thing at that level discipline. This process might take you about nine months, so now is the time to start training.

If you have already completed few races, you might be used to running two or three times per week. But you need to continue to build and increasing your miles. In the marathon training program that you choose, the long runs usually are on weekends. You can start increasing your miles until you hit 20 to 22 miles few times during the training period. These runs should be easy. For me, and some of my dear friends, we do some miles at MAF pace applying the Maffetone Method; We basically aim to stay in the aerobic range during the long runs. Dr. Maffetone gives a formula: 180 minus your age plus 5 to give you your Maximum Aerobic Function MAF pace if you are in good shape. If you keep your pace at MAF, you will be able to build up a very good aerobic base. But if for some reason you are not able to do your workout during the week, you will see that the long run during the weekend will be more difficult to do. The only time you reduce the regimen is during the last two weeks of training to taper. Remember to maintain a good nutritional diet, good rest, and get adequate sleep.

All of this is possible to accomplish by yourself. But it's better if you do it with the help of others. I don't think I couldn't ever started without the motivation of Marcela, accomplished the marathons that I have ran without the help of Coach Luis, or have made it through the long runs without the help of the Fumigaos, FIT, and my special group of Long Runs. I don't think I could have maintained the consistency of my short runs without the help of the Weston Run Club, or have improved my speed without the help of Luis Tovar. I don't think I could have improved my form without the help of Christina, kept my focus without the help of Ana Maria Villegas, or have kept my goals without the help of 1,000 Miles Challenge. We all need people. God created us this way. This book is to honor all the run clubs for bringing people with similar goals to motivate and to help each other.

God has created us to be interdependent of each other. The best way I can live is if I do something for somebody else. That is reflected even in costumer care. Rabbi Daniel Lapin talks about this in his book, "Business Secrets from the Bible" (13) (Lapin, 2014) . We need to find the area in which we can serve one another, and in developing that, we find our real race. We can become a specialist if we find the area that we are created for. I have knocked several times on the door of my friend Joaquin, a runner from Weston, to ask for help in fixing some things in my house that I am not able to do, but he can do because he is a specialist. He helps me and we both benefit from it. If we take care of all our needs alone, then we don't need one another. But that isn't God's plan. It's God's plan to help one another; that is why there are doctors, taxi drivers, bakers, and every other profession. That's why it's important to find the highest way that we can serve one another. Good businesses are those that sell products or services that enhance the lives of others, that solve their problems, and give them a better life. It's worshiping God by helping others accomplish their dreams and help them making a living so they can to take care of their families.

Biomechanics

Christina has more than five years with FIT. It has been a beautiful experience for her and a great opportunity to help others like family. Now, she is the head coach of one location and does marketing and cross promoting. She brings a lot of ideas and workshops to the table, especially in biomechanics. It's important to learn about our bodies. How do our bodies function like a machine?

Steve McCaw PhD., professor emeritus of Illinois State University, describes in his book Biomechanics for Dummies (14) (McCaw, 2014) the biomechanics of running, how the active running loads the body, the response of the body, and how different forms of running can lead to injuries. He goes on in describing that in mechanics, there are two main areas. The first is kinematics, or the description of motion. This is like when we say that person has a good form, nice pace, etc. The other is kinetics, or the forces causing motion. If you input an abnormal force, it's going to result in an abnormal change of the body in motion. The bio is related to how different tissues of the body, nerves, muscles, and bones respond to the forces imposed. The leg has three functions during locomotion: energy absorption, support, and energy generation. For absorption, the leg is like a spring or shock absorber. When the leg hits the ground, it acts like a spring being compressed to absorb energy. Then, the leg acts as support to allow rotation for the next step and lunges, acting as an energy generator.

Dr. McCaw talks about internal and external forces, the external can be caused by resistance like windy days and ground friction forces. If you find yourself hearing the scratching noises like you are dragging your feet, it's because you are creating friction forces that will waste your energy. Raise your feet. The internals are caused by changes in the body. During foot landing, the ground contact is extremely short, only a fraction of a second. During that brief time, the body is doing a lot of things. Now, the impact is more than two times of your body weight landing on your heel. This is a heavy loading, especially as the miles go by. This loading is not the same from step to step. The body deals with this by absorbing all this energy, the best way to absolve energy is by what is called the eccentric muscle activity. That means the muscle develops tension as it gets longer, also known as "giving". The way our muscles are made is to store a lot of this eccentric energy. The most controlling joint flexion that is supported by the muscles occur at the hip, then with more intensity at the knee, but even more at the ankle. This brings us to a very important muscle group. If we focus at the ankle joint, on the lateral outside front of the leg, we have the three main muscles: the tibialis anterior, the extensor digitorum longus, and the extensor hallucis longus. These muscles function to dorsiflex the foot and assist with foot eversion and inversion. On the back of our leg, we have two main muscles: the gastrocnemius and the soleus. They function to plantar flex the foot at the ankle joint and flex the leg at the knee joint.

Another way of absorption of energy is through bone micro-fractures. When a load is imposed on the bone, energy is transmitted up the bone, resulting in some of the bone giving way at a microscopic level. This little micro-fracture absorbs the energy and our body generates new bone tissue to fill the cracks. Our bones are another amazing engineering creation. The bone shape can be compared to man-made structures that hold heavy loads, such as bridges. They provide a rigid framework for support and a grid-work that is geared to mathematically respond to the loading patterns of the bone. We want to induce some micro-fractures to our bones as it stimulates our bones to make themselves stronger and prevent diseases like osteoporosis.

Dr. McCaw explains the third way energy is absorbed by our body and that is through deformation of cartilage. When bones are loaded against each other, cartilage gets compressed. Cartilage is a tremendous shock absorber that engineers have not being able to emulate. The only problem is that if cartilage gets damaged, it's very difficult to repair.

By looking at our three ways of absorbing energy, we can see that the main way we want to use to absorb energy is by our muscle eccentric energy. That is why is very important to do muscle strength exercises.

The ground reaction forces imposed to our muscles and bones have a higher impact on rear-foot runners. Looking at a mid-foot runner, the heel never makes contact with the ground, and they land on the outside portion of their foot. The impact transient of the ground reaction forces disappears. When a person lands on the rear of the foot, the ground reaction force is vector basically straight up the leg. When the person lands on the mid-foot or fore-foot, the ground reaction force is vector forward of the ankle joint and goes in direction to the back of the leg. It is not vector straight up the leg. Still, the overall loading of the body doesn't change very much. The ground reaction force is reduced greatly by a mid-foot landing, but that is only one force. There are other forces impacting our body.

Dr. McCaw also teaches about forces on the internal structures of the body. Leverage is a great way to counter-react forces. You could put a rhino on one side of a c-saw, and with enough leverage, you could put a butterfly on the other side, and the butterfly could lift the rhino. Our bone structure is a system of leverages. When forces are applied to our body, those forces cause a rotation called torque. The torque imposed by ground reaction forces need to be counter-balanced by our muscle activity. Forces imposed during a rear-foot landing are counterbalanced by front muscles called the tibialis anterior and extensors. The forces imposed when fore-foot landing are counterbalanced by the gastrocnemius and soleus. This is the real source of loading on the body. Our muscles are activated by brain signals that tell our muscles they need to provide extension. But when we are running, our brain doesn't wait until the need for extension happens. Our brain anticipates it and gives the signal before the extension happens. Basically, you are running along and the central nervous system sends a signal to produce the force according to the torque that is anticipated is going to happen. But maybe something different happens; you didn't land the way you were supposed to and the force anticipated is lower or higher than needed; this can cause an injury. As you run faster, your muscles are called to produce greater torques. Because of this, it's important to keep in mind that if you are doing a spring run, perhaps at the end of a race, you use fore-foot landing, but never rear-foot landing.

Considering all these forces and loads to the body, Dr. McCaw points out four principles of training.

- Overloading: The training load needs to go according to the fitness level. If you want to induce a training effect, tissue must be exposed to a load greater to which it has adapted. That is why the intensity needs to increase gradually, or the reason for tempo runs and speed training. In general, the higher the fitness level, the higher the training load that you can have.
- Progressive Resistance: This tells us that because adaptions are occurring, in response to an overload tissue adaptation, you need to increase or adjust your training load. When a person becomes trained, what before was a stimulating load now becomes a load that their bodies have become adopted to. Their bones have become stronger and their muscles have become stronger, so they must train to a higher level.
- Specificity: This tell us that adaptation occurs in the tissue loaded; adaptation is specific to how the tissue is loaded. You have a fitness level for specific muscles. This is important because there are exercises for the calf muscles, exercises for tibial muscles, core muscles, etc. It tells us that training has produced adaptation for specific tissues and also adapts specifically to the magnitude, the speed that you have trained for, and the range of motion that you have been used; it's not an overall improvement. For example, if you have trained your muscles, but not your cardio capacity, you may not necessarily increase your speed.
- Staying Injury Free: We know the training effects that occur by increasing your load. We also know that injuries happen, so what is the difference between training effectivity and injury? The bottom line is time.

There are two factors that contribute to training effectivity and to injuries as well. They are stress magnitude and the number of repetitions going from a single application of a level of stress, to many applications of stress levels.

Dr. McCaw indicates that there are a number of combinations between stress magnitude and repetitions that can cause an injury. For example, you can have a traumatic injury if you are running along and your twist your ankle. That is a single identifiable event that caused the injury; it was a single application of a very high level of stress that exceeds the level of tolerance where the stress was applied. On the other side of the spectrum, there are overuse injuries that are caused by cumulative loading, or when you have multiple applications of lower level of stress. So, there is a threshold between stress level and repetitions, the hard part is to identify this threshold. A paper from Keith Williams (15) (Williams, 1985) that was written over twenty years ago helps us have an idea of where this threshold is. The idea is that increased training effort leads to increased tissue stress with microscopic tissue damage. As the body responds to repair, this tissue damage gives us stronger bones and stronger muscles because there is tissue remodeling going on. When the remodeling rate is greater than the rate of damage, we are in the training effective zone. When the rate of damage is greater than the remodeling rate, we are in the injury zone. We need to give adequate time for the remodeling to occur, this will give us stronger tissues, and as our tissue get stronger, we can increase our training loads.

Dr. McCaw points these most common mistakes in training:

- Too much, too soon. We push ourselves too hard. We try to increase our speed too quickly. If you increase your distance, your body needs time to adapt. If you increase frequency, you need to do it progressively. Your body needs time to adapt. Listen to your body. If it is telling you that it needs rest, give it rest. Even if you change surface, give your body time to adapt; if you go from concrete to asphalt or sand, for example. Or if you change shoes, give your body time to adapt.
- Setting unrealistic goals. People that only run occasionally and all of the sudden want to run a marathon in two months are setting unrealistic goals.
- Running when you are tired and your muscles are fatigued.

- Don't make big changes in a single session or too soon.
- No pain, no gain is a stupid idea! Don't train through pain. When you have pain in a tissue, that is an indication that something is wrong. If you keep training, the body will compensate with other tissues for the lack of functionality of that tissue and the stress imposed on the other tissues might be too excessive. You might end up with further injuries on the compensating tissues.

In the build-up phase, we are talking about building volume. Coach Nate Helming from The Run Experience gives four important tips for the long run (16) (Pingrey, 2019), which is one of the most important trainings to build volume:

- Proper dynamic warm ups. This will help get your muscles ready with your posture and activation of your core. Nate suggests running for five minutes, then stopping and doing ten lounges, ten pushups, and ten circles per leg with four legs fully extended in a plunge position, and your hands on the floor. You need to have a mental focus on having a good mechanics throughout the long run. In a long run, you have the tendency to slump at the end. It's important to be conscious of maintaining a good posture and to wake up from the slump. He suggests every ten minutes to breath very deep through your nose and exhale though your mouth. This followed by 10 leg pulls that are more straight up, rather than butt kicks. This helps combat what he calls "marathon shuffle", or when you start dragging your feet.
- Do not run long runs too fast. The benefits from long runs come from time on your feet and steady effort, rather than speed. If we run too fast, the mechanics will go away, and the time to recover is longer.
- Stay hydrated during the run. This is regardless of the temperature or weather conditions. Even if it is raining, you need to drink water. If you are holding the water bottle in one hand, don't run the entire time holding it with the same hand. Switch hands every ten minutes or so.

My body gave me the green light to begin running but doesn't mean I can jump back into it full-force. It is important not to rush things, as patience pays off.

Luis Tovar

Photo by Luis Tovar

I believe a key factor to get faster is by increasing the pain threshold, and training as a team will help us tolerate more pain. There is rarely a speed workout when we don't feel we want to stop, because speed hurts. Sometimes we even start thinking of an excuse to stop and cut it short. However, knowing we have people around us going through the same pain makes us tolerate it more and instead of stopping we push.

Ana Maria Villegas

Photo by Ana Maria Villegas

Do what you love to do and you'll never have a
problem with Monday.

Ana Maria Villegas

Chapter 3.
SPEED TRAINING

Running Economy

As you improve, you need to be prepared for new changes. It was in kilometer 23 of the Berlin Marathon when I felt a snap on my soleus in my left leg. The pain was so intense that I had to look for a first aid station and ask the volunteers to give me a quick massage. The rest of the race I was limping. Still, I completed the race in 4 hours and 16 minutes. But if I would do the plan, as my coach Luis showed me, I easily could break the four hours. I ran too fast the first half and the oxygen demand was higher for the overwork of the muscles and boom, I had a cramp. I ran with poor running economy. When I came back, I explained the situation to Christina Quadra. She guided me to do exercises to recuperate and to gain muscle strength and to improve my form.

Jeff Galloway, author of "Marathon you can do it!" and "Galloway's Book on Running" is the designer of the Galloway Program; it's made for people that want to finish strong doing a running/walking Marathon. Mr. Galloway started his Run Walk/Run Method in 1974 (17) (Galloway, 1984). He opened a running store and decided to take some customers to run, although many of them were not in shape for long running. After a few training sessions around the track, he discovered that walking breaks were crucial for them to be able to finish a 5k or 10k. His focus was on their breathing rate, and if somebody was breathing too hard, they would need to walk more or slow their pace. Run-Walk-Run is a form of interval training. According to Mr. Galloway, the method helps improve finish times, gives runners control over fatigue, and is a smart way to run. The walk/run interval, more than a rest, is a way to stabilize the aerobic heart rate and will make you feel like you are resting. It is important to keep a strong walk pace, maybe between 15 to 18 minutes per mile, to keep a good heart rate.

Something that I like about running is that you can measure if you are getting better. That measure can be distance, time, or frequency. I can choose any of the three, or all of them, and decide how to improve, or see if I am getting better. Human nature wants to see improvement. When the body gets used to a certain routine, it starts asking you for more, a better technique, more distance, or more speed. I think it's this way in all aspects of our life. We want to know more or get better in our jobs – we simply want to be better. Some of my friends from FIT started running at a pace of 11, 12, or 13 minutes per mile, and now they are running at 8, 9, or 10 minutes per mile. They feel there is an improvement. I am no saying that you need to become super-fast to be good. Your body reacts to your pace, and when you become faster, it's because your capacity has increased. It's not the same running 13 minutes pace and running 10 minutes pace. It's not the same walking 18 minutes pace and walking 15 minutes pace. When your body is telling you that speed is your limit, you don't need to force it. Now you can add distance. It's not the same to run a 10k as a half marathon, or a full marathon. And if you feel that you reach your distance limit, you can add frequency. But again, it's not the same running only once a week, 10 miles per week, 20 miles per week, or 30 miles per week.

During your off-season training is a good time to focus on strength. In United States, the main races are between August and March. People prepare for these races with structured plans. The time between your last race and the preparation for the next one is a good time to create balance, strengthen your muscles, focus on fitness, and reboot your system. During this time, you can cut the volume down and pay more attention to form. It is also a good time to do routines and exercises that will help you to increase speed and efficiency.

Running economy is a measure of efficiency. When a car runs more efficiently, it gets more mileage with the least amount of fuel usage. Our fuel is oxygen and our running economy is how efficiently we use oxygen to run more. Running economy is the amount of oxygen that we use relative to body weight and speed. When the body is not running efficiently, maybe due to unnecessary motions, there is an increase of oxygen demand and running economy is poor. We can express running economy by the velocity achieved for a specific oxygen consumption rate, or by the specific VO2 needed to maintain a certain speed. For the body to have a physiological adaptation, the training needs to be done at an appropriate intensity.

In an article, Dr. Philo Saunders from the department of physiology of the Australian Institute of Sport, talks about Running Economy (RE) (18) (Saunders, 2004), and says that taking in consideration body mass, runners with good RE use less energy and therefore less oxygen that runners with poor RE running at the same velocity. Essentially, they are more efficient. Furthermore, he says that there is a strong association between RE and distance running. There are few factors that can affect RE including metabolic adaptations, strength training and altitude training. When I run in Bogota, it takes time to adapt and the altitude makes you a more efficient runner, I notice a big change when I run in Florida when I get back. I feel like flying. No wonder why athletes that train in high altitudes are more efficient. But there's little that we can do about it when we live at sea-level. On the other hand, strength training allows the muscles to utilize more elastic energy and reduce the amount of energy wasted in braking forces. But something we can do about it is concentrating on making strengthening exercise a part of our habits.

Speed training can increase your aerobic capacity, improve your running economy, and make your running more efficient. Intervals and tempo runs are the most popular forms of speed work. Intervals are a set of repetitions of a specific, short distances, ran at a substantially faster pace than usual with recovery jogs in between. For example, you might run four, one-mile repeats at a hard pace, with five minutes slow jogging, or even walking between the mile repeats. Tempo runs are longer than an interval, generally in the range of 4–10 miles, depending on where you are in your training, but they must be at a challenging and sustainable pace. This kind of workout teaches your body, as well as your brain, to sustain challenging work over a longer period of time. Always allow your body to warm up and cool down with a few easy miles at the beginning and end of any speed workout. It is very important to allow time for rest and recovery. This means no running. You can do some cross-training like cycling or swimming. Swimming is very good for your breathing and can help you tremendously. In the two weeks prior to the race, it's important to scale back on your mileage and to let your body rest for the race. It's good to change surfaces from time to time, go for runs on asphalt, sometimes on dirt roads, or the beach, on grass, or sometimes even the treadmill to help with speed.

Kaizen

Carlos, a 69-year-old runner from Brazil just run the Tokyo Marathon finishing with a net time of 3:55. Carlos runs like he is 30 and is an example and source of motivation to many runners. Tokyo was his 6th major marathon, making him the recipient of the Six Star World Majors Medal. He loved Japan; Japan is an example of a winning nation. The country rose up from a time of suffering and defeat. Japan itself is a country that went through big transformations. During the marathon of Tokyo, you can feel those transformations. You can see the old and the new. The race starts by the Tokyo Metropolitan Government Building, where the big decisions are made in this part of the world. Kyoto is the former capital of Japan and is the best place to see the old and traditional Japanese culture. Kyoto is famous for its classical temples, gardens, and imperial palaces. The marathon passes by the Shinjuku station, the busiest train station in the world. 2019 was the year for the 12th Tokyo Marathon, and just last year, 30,000 people participated from the 300,000+ that applied. Running through the marathon will expose you to the history, tradition and culture of Japan. Many representative musical groups and dancers are performing along the route. In Tokyo, you can see places like the Meiji Shrine, a very traditional place that is almost 100 years old. You can also see Akihabara, the Anime and Manga capital of the world, and the meeting place of the Otaku (Manga Fan). Then, you pass by Asakusa, the low City of Tokyo. It's a place full of temples. The race crosses the Sumita River, which is close to the Skytree, the tallest building in Japan. Shibuya is the light city of Tokyo and the Tsukiji market are two places that I must see when I visit. And finally, the Imperial Palace is the finish line.

I asked one of my friends that went to Tokyo what she liked most. She said the toilets. Toilets in Japan are unique, fully automated, with control panels that have more buttons than a TV remote control. They have buttons for wash, sprays for O-Shiri (your rear), a bidet which is for ladies. There are buttons to stop the wash, to air dry, to flush, to heat the seat, to warm the water, and if you have time to read something, you even have a button for a massage.

Every time I think of Japan, I think about one word: Kaizen. In the 1950s, buying something made in Japan meant buying something of very poor quality. In those years when you heard about Japanese made products, you associated those to the cheapest products you could find. But now, products made in Japan are of very high quality. When you think of Japan, brands like Toyota, Yamaha, Sony, and Motorola may come to your mind. But what happened? How those bad products turned into the great products that we know. The answer is Kaizen, a Japanese word that means continuous improvement. They idea of improving initially means to eliminate things that are delaying the improvement. Quality control managers call it waste. It can be related to something material, to a process, or to time. For example, if I must repeat something because I am doing it wrong, then I am losing time, and that is waste.

Kaizen also means "change for better". As I build my running capacity, I am changing, and for the better. I can relate this to everything I do in life. The question that I need to answer every day is, what can I do today that is better than yesterday? It doesn't matter if it's just a very small change or a big change. What is important is to not to stay in the same place. Kaizen is a lean methodology that uses tools like Kaizen events. If I do a Kaizen event in my life, I need to monitor a process that I do. For instance, something like a habit is something done in the way that I am used to doing it, but also seeing how I can improve it. Just a small example, I notice that I am always late for my practice and this might disturb the schedule of others in my group. Someone might need to leave quickly to take a child to school and can be impacted if practice starts late. So, how can I improve this? Perhaps I can get up 15 minutes earlier. I could leave everything out the night before. As for another example, if I am not communicating the right way in front of people, maybe I should get a coach, do exercises, or join toast masters.

In running, I can relate Kaizen to many things. If I don't pay attention to warming up or stretching, I can end up injured, and that's going to take time away from my running and resources if I pay for medical attention. Or, if I run with shoes that are not appropriate, then I may end up paying more for new shoes when I could be saving. Building up means to continuously improve and to become a more efficient runner. One of the most important aspects of eliminating waste is running economy, this is the demand for a sub-maximal running and the efficient use of oxygen, which can be measured by the max steady-state consumption of oxygen (VO2 Max) and the respiratory exchange ratio.

When things are more efficient, they can go faster, and speed can be added. A more efficient runner is a faster runner. I can relate this to anything in life. For instance, aviation is an industry that has grown tremendously since its humble beginnings, and in a relative short time. The more efficient the airplanes became, the faster the industry grew. The development of such technology is exponential. We know more in the last 20 years than probably the entire last century. This is thanks to people that lived and ran their race. The Wright brothers went through many setbacks, disappointments, frustrations, criticism, and obstacles. But thanks to their determination, I can leave on a trip to Tokyo and be there the next day. One of the most wonderful inventions, like the airplane, came to be due to their failures, frustrations, and disappointments. Kaizen is continuous improvement. It is to be better and to do better. But more than that, it's to have a dream, a purpose, and a goal in mind. Thomas Edison, one of the most genius minds in the world, had thousands of failures trying to invent the light bulb. For him, they were not failures, they were unsuccessful attempts. Thomas Edison said, "I haven't failed. I've just found 10,000 ways that won't work." Edison was running his race. He fell more than 10,000 times, but he got up and kept going. He accomplished his dream and crossed the finish line. When Edison's plant burned down and was engulfed in flames, he told his son "Go and tell your mother and all her friends. They'll never see a fire like this!" Later he said, "Although I am over 67 years old, I'll start all over again tomorrow." We may fall one, two, three times, ten thousand times, but that doesn't mean we are not getting better. We fall, we get up, we learn, we keep going, and those falls are part of getting better.

A Mentor, A Coach

God created us with an instinct to advance. If you are crawling, you want to walk. If you have a starter house, you want a better house. We were created with a desire to do better. We want to go farther and we want to go faster. Speed is a product of efficiency; it comes with it. It is natural that as we run more, we get stronger. We become more efficient, faster, and we build more volume. I really enjoy seeing other friends change with time; their training and consistency starts paying off. In Florida, there is a race that is very fun, one of the most fun races that I have been to. I am referring to the Keys 100. It's a race from Key Largo to Key West. It has two categories: individual and team relays. Last year, we put together a team with the very fast people of FIT and called it FITOPIA as an allegory of the movie Zootopia (19) (Howard, 2016). The relay consisted of a team of six and rented a very nice van. Each runner runs about 3 to 5 miles at a time, then transfers the baton to the next runner and so on until the 100 miles are covered. We laugh, dance, and share beautiful moments of the 12:30 hours of racing. Marina is the star of the team. She is super-fast and is like the gazelle of the movie. Bryan is tall as the bull in the movie and has deep focus while running. Christy is very sweet and full of energy like the bunny in the movie. Joe has the form of an ultra-marathoner and is not even close to the sloth in the movie. I am fast, maybe because of the lack of hair, so all the opposites of the camel with its huge mane. Luis Tovar is the fastest of the group, and as swift as the fox of the movie. In the last race, I had the opportunity to meet so many people, among them Ana Maria Villegas, one of the fastest runners in South Florida, and a runner that I admire for her dedication and love for the sport.

Ana Maria is from Colombia, began running, let's say with certain structure, about five years ago. After her daughter's second birthday, she felt the need and desire to become a healthier person. Like many of us, she started to run maybe one or two miles. Thanks to her determination, and the help of her group, she is where she is right now, a sub-three hour marathoner, two-time female champion of Wings for Life Run in USA and in Australia, several times finisher of the Boston Marathon with a PR of 2:52, not to mention many other accomplishments. Her first marathon was in Chicago where she qualified for Boston; that was only her first marathon! It has not been easy, though. Ana has made huge adjustments to keep balance in what is important in her life like family, work, and her passion for running. The key of having success is balance.

Many times, we need to make adjustments that require sacrifice, discipline, a different mindset, and habits to have balance. It doesn't mean to give up on something that is important for us, it means making it work. Ana Maria has been able to follow a very structured training program and her advice, especially for women, is to be very organized, keep the goal in mind, and to make the sacrifices that imply. To get to the level of commitment that Ana has, it doesn't happen overnight. It takes time, but it's better to do it in stages. When we need changes in our life, it's important to start with something and start adding new changes over the ones already established; that is Kaizen in action. Initially, habits demand sacrifice, but when they are followed, they become part of life. First, we let our choices establish the habits, and later, we let the habits establish our choices, which brings structure to our lives. Like Ana says, this is a message that we want to pass on to our children and to the people that we have an influence on. The habit brings discipline and needs to come to a point that if you don't do it, you are missing something, your day is not good, or is out of place.

Ana really likes the sport and wants to advance more, and it's much easier with the support of others. When she started, sometimes she would see the groups of people from different running clubs sharing the road and having a good time. This motivated her to find people that share her same passion. She found the group of iRun, a very recognized group internationally and in Florida; they brought a new atmosphere to her training. When she wanted to run faster, she stuck to the fastest runners, and that became her inner group within the group. We all need people that will push us to be better and mentors that will share their wisdom with us. For Ana, there are two special people that have helped her in a very special way: her friend Michelle and her coach, Cobi. When we have people that go side-by-side with us, we can go farther. Ana has three people in her group that are key for her hard trainings, as it is very encouraging to have somebody on your side that you know is doing the same effort, suffering as you are, and keeps you going. Michelle is a special person for Ana, she admires her because she balances a very busy life with a family of five children, work, a sport, and many other things. Yet, she has makes things work with sacrifice and discipline.

The people that have being through the same things that we have are the best to support us. We can also best support those that are going through the same things we have. It is our testimony that can make a difference. We can serve those better that we have sympathy for. We have a message we can share; we can help others to cross the finish line. Who else more important to share our message than to our children? What Ana wants to share with her two beautiful girls is a message of love, the importance of the discipline, dedication, and the power of the mind. Ana mentions how a marathon compared to our life is like a journey, and we might get to a point in the race when there are no more legs, no even more heart, and what the only thing left is our mind. Like the race, we might have good days, bad days, and even worse days. If that happens, we need to evaluate our thinking, renew our mind, be strong-minded, and realize that tomorrow is going to be a better day. We only go through hard things temporarily. Like in a marathon, I might feel bad in this mile, but in the next, I might feel better. And eventually, I am going to recover and feel better. For example, if we are running and you start feeling tired in the mile 18, but if you see in your mind that it's too hard, you might not finish. Then, you won't finish because your mind is already getting the idea that you won't make it. We need to see the goal, concentrate in the moment and believe that we can do the impossible. Ana never though that she would be able to run a marathon; she barely ran one or two miles. For her, it was an impossible. But she believed herself to be a runner that could run a marathon under 3:00 hours, and she did it.

I can't write about speed without mentioning "El Maestro," Eliud Kipchoge (20) (Cathal, 2016), the greatest marathoner ever. He had won nine straight marathons, an Olympic Gold medal, and set the world record with an outstanding 2:01:39 in Berlin 2017. Eliud, from Kenya is a man of great discipline. He gets up every morning at 5:00 am for his morning runs and records every single workout in a note book, and has probably has more than 15 notebooks now. The man of great wisdom once said, "Only the disciplined ones in life are free. If you are undisciplined, you are a slave to your moods and your passions." He also said, "It's not about the legs; it's about the heart and the mind." Many people including David Bedford, organizer of the

London Marathon and former 10,000 meters world-record holder, believes he can be the greatest distance runner ever. He has excellent nutrition habits and never had an injury.

Eliud, a man of humble beginnings from the village of Kapsisiywa, Kenya, had to run to school every day. He helped his family by collecting milk from his friends and neighbors and sold it in the market. He was inspired by Patrick Sang, a runner of his home town, who went to the University of Texas and won an Olympic Silver medal. When Sang returned to the town, he helped Eliud, and became a mentor to him. At that time, Eliud was 16. Sang gave him training plans and even gave him his own watch because Eliud could not afford one. Patrick once said, "When you're young, you always hope that one day you'll be somebody and, in that journey, you need someone to hold you by the hand. It does not matter who that person is, so long as they believe that your dreams are valid. So, for me, when you find a young person with a passion, don't disappoint them. Give them a helping hand and see them grow."

Eliud has an incredible average pace of 4:36 for the marathon, although his dream has been to finish a marathon under 2 hours. He participated in the project organized by Nike called "Breaking 2" (21) (Nike, 2019) in which he got a time of 2:00:25; he was only 25 seconds short of becoming probably the only one, now and ever, to run a marathon under 2:00. But still his time is the fastest time that any human being has achieved in the marathon distance, even though it's not an official world record.

Kenya is a country that produces some of the world's best runners. Kenya has 42 ethnic tribes; the Kalenjin tribe is one of those with a of about 4.9 million. Within this tribe, the Nandi subgroup is the region that has produced almost all long-distance running champions. Many think the reason for this is a combination of high altitudes, genes, lifestyle, food, and environment. I visited Kenya in 1992 and went to Kitale, a village in the Nandi region. I went for helicopter training in one of the Helimission Bases. We landed in one pinnacle of about 10,000 feet, and from there, we could see Lake Victoria and the Great Rift Valley. The view was beautiful, and filled with rolling hills and red soiled roads where many Kenyans run. Kids that run to school every day become the best long-distance runners. Genes are noticed in their long legs, big chest, and low-fat index. Their lifestyle and culture are surrounded by the sport; running to Kenyans is like soccer to Brazilians. Motivation is a mix of love for running and desire to have a better financial life. The Kenyan runners' food is from the farm, and I believe, we all should try to eat as closest to food picked from the ground as possible. The food is rich in good carbohydrates, fiber, and protein. They eat a lot of vegetables and is one mainly of only organic food. One dish loved by runners in Kenya is Ugali, a traditional dish made from ground maize that is cooked to a mashed potato-like texture. An observation on the diet of elite African runners is one mainly from Ethiopia that consists of a high percentage of carbohydrates in the form of staples, rice, lintels, porridge, and vegetables. Carbohydrates are good for storing glycogen, fueling performance, and defense from injuries. The difference between eating carbohydrates in America and eating carbohydrates in Kenya by runners is the rate of burning. Injera is the staple of Ethiopia, Ugali the staple of Kenya and is equivalent, arepas and tamales for the Latins, and oats in America. Brown rice offers an addition to the carbohydrates: fiber. Quinoa is a great gluten-free source of amino acids and iron-rich carbohydrates. It's very important to have good fuel to push the afterburners of the engines for fast running.

The environment in Kenya is perfect for running. The open roads are good for the feet, there are race tracks in training camps or in the middle of the village, and the climate is great. They also have good coaches like Brother Colm O'Connell (22) (Firstpost, 2012), an Irish coach who has worked in Kenya for more than 25 years and who teaches the value of exercises and the value of different types of training. Coach O'Connell uses the acronym FAST to make runners run faster; F is for Focus, A for Alignment, S for Stability and T for Timing your tempo with the ground. Kenyan runners trained by Coach O'Connell start their training programs by running slow. They do aerobic runs so they can concentrate on technique and form. They do exercises to build muscle. Their trainings are not intense but relaxing. They learn to focus, to put aside distractions, wobbly legs, keep their heads down to distractions. They almost lock into position even before the race starts and run in control. They have structure in the training and every workout has a purpose. It might look like they are living in a fantasy, but there is a time when they must go back to realty, and face the race they all have. Many Kenyan runners see a way to liberty of prosperity thought running. Many come from poor rural areas, and their reality is that every step is bringing them closer to the goal. Every step is the difference between a present with difficulties, or a life with freedom from poverty. This is how we need to face life, like if every step we take can become closer to our dream.

The training is behind, now focus on the race. Don't give up, the pain of regret for no finishing is worse than the pain you might have when you cross the finish line.

Luis Tovar

Photo by Luis Tovar

The one who does not give in, the one who endures, even embraces the pain, is the one who reaches the goal.

Ana Maria Villegas

Photo by Ana Maria Villegas

We have fun, we help each other, we build community, we motivate each other, we run our race, and we wait for others when they cross the finish line.

Photo by Ana Mary Guillen

Chapter 4.
THE RACE

26.2

Among a multitude of people, we listen the National Anthem and know the culmination of many months of preparation are going to pay off in the race that is about to start. All the workouts, tempos, speed trainings, early rises, and long runs are in the past. We are better because of the training, but we need to leave it behind and focus on the race. Another race will come that will require new training, but if we are standing on the start line, we need to put our minds in the 26.2-mile journey to the finish line. Sometimes we look at our past and we don't leave it behind. We let our past give direction to our lives. But we have something bigger to look at ahead. Maybe all those days or preparation were intense and long, but the race is something bigger. Like Coach O'Connel said, "To win the race you need to lock your focus on what is going ahead." When I drive my car, I look what is in front of the windshield, that is where I am going.

What is in the small mirror is what is behind. I cannot control where I am going just by looking at the mirror. You cannot have control of your life just by what's in the past. Ok, maybe the present is not what we would like it to be. Maybe we don't know how where we are going to go in the present. Things may not look so good. No matter what has happened, no matter if you or one of your loved ones succumbed to a sickness, no matter if your children were victims of abuse, no matter if your best friend committed suicide, God is going to bring you truth. You might be wondering if the sun is going to come out again, but I'll tell you God can carry us through anything. He will run the race with us, he will be our source of strength, and he will take us through the finish line. The race is here, we are going to win it, even before the race starts. Our mind will be locked in our goal. Maybe you look at the past and you feel tired, maybe look at your present and you feel tired, but there is nothing wrong with feeling tired. What is wrong is to not finish, to throw the towel, to give up, and that my friend requires fighting.

If I look at the past, maybe it will be to run the marathon in Athens and be able to see where everything started. It was 490 BC when Pheidippides, a Greek soldier, ran from a battle field near the town of Marathon to Athens carrying the very important message that the Greek army had defeated the Persians. The distance between the two towns was 42 kilometers, or 26.2 miles. He delivered the message "Niki" [Victory!], and then he died.

Although Pheidippides died, nobody in good health dies from running a marathon; And you know what? Women can run a marathon! Many didn't think that way. The first woman that ran the Boston marathon had to do it in disguise. When Roberta "Bobbi" Gibb found out at the age of 23 that her entry to the Boston Marathon was denied, she decided to run it anyway. She received a letter on the mail from the race director saying, "This is an AAU Men's Division race only. Women are not allowed, and furthermore are not physiologically able." He also made a comment on TV that women's physiological constitution made them capable to only run three to five miles. Gibb finished the Boston marathon in 3:21:40 wearing a swimsuit, Bermuda shorts, and boy's running shoes. She wore her brother's hoody and hid in the bushes near the start line.

When the race started, she let the fast runners go by and then jumped from the bushes to slip into the middle of the pack. She finished the race with blisters and was bleeding for wearing boy's running shoes because they were not for women. She traveled 3,000 miles from her home in San Diego to run the race, but most importantly because if she didn't finish, she was to set women's running 20, 30 years back. They'd say, "See? That's why we don't let women run these long distances." So, she had to finish. Those were the words of Bobbie; she wouldn't let that happen and that was her real race and purpose in life at that time.

The second woman that ran the Boston Marathon was the first one to run it with a participant number, which made her the first official female participant. But she also had to disguise. She had to register with her name in a way that didn't show it was a female name. When Katherine Switzer started the race, she blended among the other participants with short hair and wearing the 261 bib. Katherine was running the race when an official spotted her, realizing she was a woman. He jumped from a bus, grabbed her, and tried to push her away saying, "Get the hell out of my race." Fortunately, her boyfriend tackled the guy, sending him against the bushes opening the way for Katherine to finish the race. The incident brought the attention of the race organizers and made it possible for women to run Boston and many other marathons.

The first woman that ran a marathon in the USA was actually not Bobbie or Katherine, it was Arlene Pieper. My friend Marcela told me about her because she had the honor to meet her in person. Arlene ran the Pikes Peak Marathon which never banned women from racing. In 1959, Arlene ran the full marathon that was thought could never be accomplished by a woman because of its toughness. Arlene didn't know about her accomplishment as the first female marathoner in the US until decades after the race. People were looking for her to tell her about what she accomplished. A reward was posted in a newspaper for the person that would find her. Finally, she was found and she was recognized for what she did.

For me the race, is The Race, and The Race is The Boston Marathon. This race is hard, because is supposed to be hard. It is hard to run it, it is hard to get in. The only way to participate in this race is if you qualify, or if you raise funds for a charity. The Boston Marathon is the oldest annual marathon run in the USA and possibly of the world. It's also one of the most prestigious races. The first-time runners line up to run the Boston Marathon was in April 19, 1897. Since then, all runners have talked about the most challenging mile, the Heartbreak Hill, where a statue of Jonny A Kelley was erected. The person that runs more Boston's Marathons than any other was Johnny Kelley, who ran it 61 times. From 1934 to 1950, he finished in the top with times in the 2:30s. His last Marathon was in 1992 at the age of 84. Besides being the "Runner of the Century", Johnny was an artist. He painted more than 20 paintings a year, the most commissioned of them was titled "The Boston Dream". At age 70, Johnny said, "I'm afraid to stop running. I feel too good. I want to stay alive." Johnny, two-times Olympian, passed away in 2004.

Some tips and strategy to run Boston Marathon from Mario Fraioli (23) (Dos Santos, 2014), coach at Ekiden:

- Be prepared for the process of the start, which will take time before you get to the start line.
- The first 5k is the fastest of the race and it's very easy to be carried away. Try to relax and treat it like a warm up.
- Pay attention to the weather and account for what is happening ahead of time.
- The race is net downhill. There are some hills, so train for the shift of hills in the last 5 miles when you will use other muscles.
- Try to know what pace to expect downhill and uphill. You will probably lose some seconds that you need to recuperate during the downhill.
- Practice on the long runs what you need for the race, eating and drinking schedule, not only for Boston, but in general.

Nothing Can Stop Us...

Luis Tovar, another friend that ran with us in Keys 100, is the fastest runner in FIT. He just qualified for Boston with a time of 2:55:05. He wasn't a runner three years ago with a weight of 202 pounds. Luis almost quit running with FIT because he was going through some difficulties. But thanks to our friend Marcela and her support, Luis continued. But this time, he had a new determination to change, a new diet, and new goals. He became one of the greatest runners in South Florida.

Luis came from Venezuela and started from zero. In Caracas, Luis wanted to run, but unfortunately the area where he lived was too dangerous and nobody run outside. When Luis came to the USA and found a new family in FIT, he met many people, and now we have great respect and admiration for him. His photography is a beautiful artistic display of his passion for running. He kept on training and when he ran his first race and was surprised to find out that he was first place in his category. That was his motivation. He knows he can do this and that he can get better in each race, not necessarily to win, but to see continuous improvement. Kaizen.

Like Ana Maria, something that helped Luis a lot was to run with people faster than him. In this case, Luis met Max, another great runner. They used each other's synergy for improvement and together a half marathon side-by-side. Both finished at 1:29. When Luis ran the next half, he did it in less than 6:30 pace. But like he said, his body was not yet fully trained to run this speed and had some pain at the end that made him take a long break. Luis said that everyone must have his or her own experience. We can all train, we can all plan, but everyone's experience is different. I would say that the route set for us in different and unique ways, as we are all unique and cannot live in the other person's experience. We need to be happy for those that are doing well, and we need to support those that are not doing so well. Whatever I am dealing with, it's part of my experience and I must go through it. Thanks be to God that He is always on our side.

Every Boston marathon is a different experience. There were times when it was so hot that people went out to cheer with hoses to spray water on the runners. It was a real challenge to stay in the race of 2017 with a very high temperature. In the Boston Marathon, there are 29 medical tents along the route and 7,000 volunteers to assist the race. But that particular year, it was so hot that the 29 stations were full. It was so hot that extra wheel chairs where popping up to attend the overly-dehydrated runners. The race of 2018 was the opposite. Many runners started with normal clothes for a normal race, but the temperature dropped so much. For Ana Maria Villegas, the Boston Marathon of 2018 was an experience like no other. She mentioned that her preparation was by the book. She paid attention to her nutrition and mental attitude, but the day of the race, she encountered weather conditions that she didn't expect. She knew that was going to be cold and it was going to rain, but what she felt was much more intense of what the prognostics said. In spite of the several layers she was wearing, she felt an intense cold, plus her shoes were wet. Before the start, her group, like others, tried to stay close to warm each other. She had so much pain in her fingers and toes that she couldn't understand how she was going to be able to run. The race hadn't started yet and she already had such pain. The adrenaline helped her to start and everything was good for the first 13-15 miles. But suddenly the cold increased and her body just shut down. She couldn't feel her toes, she though that her toes were going to break, for a while she didn't have any sensitivity in her legs. She couldn't stop shaking. At that Moment her race turned into her fight, she had to fight, to never stop, to keep moving forward, at whatever pace. Like any other Marathon was a fight to cross the line, it wasn't to do PR, just to finish and even though, she finished at 3:11, it was a tuff battle, but she won, she crossed the finish line. Things sometimes turn around on us, you prepare, you plan, you anticipated, have a plan A, plan B and plan C, you expect the best, but suddenly the conditions changed. The deal fell through, the person didn't show up, the line stopped before you made it, the answer was no. You know, is a battle, you haven't loosed the fight. Maybe the pain is so intense that you feel you can't take one more single step, come on, keep going, you can do it. You will cross the finish line. Ana Maria did it, she was shaken, didn't feel her legs, but she did it. You can do it; God will give you the extra breath that you need. You will cross the finish line.

The rain, the cold, and the wind really affected the runners during the 2018 race. Many of the elites abandoned it. Probably what it got the finishers through was the other's suffering was the same; misery likes company. Well, there is the pain of the skin, there is the pain of the bone, but there is nothing like the pain of the heart. The only way I can describe this is when I got the news that my mom, at the age of 48, was involved in a vehicle accident with my sister. Vicky, my sister, made it with some fractures, but my mom didn't make it. And it was all because an irresponsible driver decided to hit the road under the influence of alcohol. Maybe the same feeling of many with a pain without description for what happened on the bombing of the Boston Marathon, where so many lives were lost and affected because of an irresponsible person.

One day in February of 2018, Runners Depot wanted to share a heart of solidarity with the victims and the families of a shooting that took place in Parkland, Florida. They were expecting a few people and we were going to run to the Stoneman Douglas High School. Instead of few people, hundreds of people showed up at the parking lot to offer love and respect. We started running at dawn, and as the sun was going down the horizon, we reached the school with an orange sky that turned into night. The feeling was like being on sacred ground. The pictures of young people along the fence with flowers and signs of messages that came from the bottom of the heart was a sign for sadness and solidarity. A moment of silence and prayers for the families went to heaven as an aroma of incense filled the air.

One Sunday morning in November of 2018, a group of bicyclists were doing their weekend routine along highway 84 in Davie Florida, living their passion, and having fun with friends. Suddenly, a driver that was distracted ran into the group. One woman lost her life and the next day another member of the group died in the hospital. Others were sent to intensive care. Only because of a driver that wasn't paying attention. It was so painful for us to see others suffering doing the same thing that we do. Like this, there are thousands of stories that you might know. For a moment, we shift the focus from ourselves, and somehow transport our spirit to be with the suffering and their families.

We would like to be there and tell them that they are not alone. And that is what happens, you are not alone, and God is on your side.

Many lives have been lost in my country of Colombia at the hands of irresponsible people that tried to enforce their ideology with a weapon in their hand. But Colombia didn't let that stop her. I didn't let that irresponsibility that killed my mom stopped me. The students of Stoneman Douglas didn't let sorrow stop them. Ana Maria didn't let the cold, the rain, or the pain stop her. Luis didn't let the pain stop him and the Boston runners didn't let the tragedy stop them. Life is precious and we need to have respect it. We need to make a better place for us to live and we need to count our blessings. We need to live our lives to the fullest and not let anything stop us.

These inserts from President Obama's speech in response to the bombing in the Boston Marathon are beautiful expressions honoring the victims of the tragedy. The city of Boston, the determination of the runners, the heart of the American people, and the human spirit of resilience: "Scripture tells us to run with endurance the race that has set before us. On Monday morning, the sun rose over Boston. The sunlight glistened off the State House Dome. In the commons, in the public garden, spring was in bloom. On this Patriot's Day, like so many before, fans jumped onto the T to see the Sox at Fenway. In Hopkinton, runners laced up their shoes and set out on a 26.2-mile test of dedication and grit and the human spirit. And across this city, hundreds of thousands of Bostonians lined the streets to hand the runners cups of water, to cheer them on. It was a beautiful day to be in Boston, a day that explains why a poet once wrote that this town is not just a capital, not just a place. Boston, he said, is the perfect state of grace.... And then, in an instant, the day's beauty was shattered. A celebration became a tragedy. And so, we come together to pray and mourn and measure our loss. But we also come together today to reclaim that state of grace, to reaffirm that the spirit of this city is undaunted, and the spirit of the country shall remain undimmed.... In the words of Dick Hoyt, who has pushed his disabled son Rick in 31 Boston marathons, we can't let something like this stop us. This doesn't stop us. And that's what you've taught us, Boston.... That's what you've reminded us, to push on, to persevere, to not grow weary, to not get faint even when it hurts. Even when our heart aches, we summon the strength that maybe we didn't even know we had, and we carry on; we finish the race. We finish the race, and we do that because of who we are, and we do that because we know that somewhere around the bend, a stranger has a cup of water. Around the bend, somebody's there to boost our spirits. On that toughest mile, just when we think that we've hit a wall, someone will be there to cheer us on and pick us up if we fall. We know that.... We carry on. We race. We strive. We build and we work, and we love, and we raise our kids to do the same. And we come together to celebrate life and to walk our cities and to cheer for our teams when the Sox, then Celtics, then Patriots or Bruins are champions again, to the chagrin of New York and Chicago fans. The crowds will gather and watch a parade go down Boylston Street. And this time next year on the third Monday in April, the world will return to this great American city to run harder than ever and to cheer even louder for the 118th Boston Marathon. Bet on it. Tomorrow the sun will rise over Boston. Tomorrow the sun will rise over this country that we love, this special place, this state of grace. Scripture tells us to run with endurance the race that is set before us. As we do, may God hold close those who've been taken from us too soon, may he comfort their families, and may he continue to watch over these United States of America."

The beautiful words of president Obama describe the heart of the runner in life and on the road. It describes the race of those that have come before us to pave the way for a better future of our children. In moments of frustration, disappointment, despair, pain, or setback, nothing can stop us from finishing the race.

Hop On

Marathon participants are increasing worldwide. In the US alone, over half a million marathon finishers registered last year. Motivation to run a marathon can be because it is a life changing event for somebody, a victory of overcoming a personal challenge, or to identify with a cause. Running can teach you that we can do hard things and that it's worth it. He says that the best thing about a marathon race is to maximize our own potential. The body can perform three times what we had trained for and really the main battle is in the mind. If somebody else wins, it doesn't mean I have a bad performance. And if I win, it doesn't mean I have a good performance. The key is that we have a potential that we can maximize, and that is our goal.

We can use the people around us to elevate us to new levels and we can help to elevate them, as professor Ward puts it. When we focus on being the best I can be is when we reach our highest potential. I remember when I started running, I mentioned to somebody close to me that I wanted to run a marathon. The reaction that I got from that person was that I was a crazy, it was impossible for me to do that, that only well-trained people can do that, and I never was going to be even be closer to even run a 10k, much less a marathon. Don't believe people that try to push you down and say that you cannot make your dreams come true.

Many roads around the world are the playground of thousands of runners, as around the world running has experienced a huge boom of popularity. In Spain, there are breath-taking landscapes and is home to great marathons like the Bilbao Night Marathon and the Minorca Cami de Cavalls Epic 360 degrees trail. The Minorca Cami is one of the longest and hardest races in Europe with 158 km. In Colombia, many people take advantage of the Ciclovia on Sundays when the main roads of the cities are closed and turned into a major running road; the climb in Bogota to "Los Patios" with a gain of 2,000 feet in elevation is a great challenge. In Brazil, especially in Rio running has boomed since Rio hosted the Olympics. People go to the beach and run along the promenade, Ipanema or Copa cabana. The Tijuca Forest in the hills West of Rio has trails that pass waterfalls and is full of monkeys and other wildlife with views of the city and the Jesus [Christ the Redeemer] statue on Corcovado. There are trails from the forest to the base of the statue.

According to Active the best 10 cities for runners in USA (24) (Grotewold, 2019) are,

- Washington DC with a vibrant community of running clubs like DC Road Runners, the Marine Corps Marathon, and places to run like the Mall.
- Flagstaff, Arizona is a training camp at 7,000 feet above sea level and is home of the McMillan Elite a group coached by Greg MacMillan.
- Minneapolis/St. Paul, Minnesota, with the most beautiful urban marathon, the "Twin Cities Marathon". It's home of Team USA Minnesota, with trails like the chain of lakes or 24 indoor running tracks.
- San Francisco, California, with places to run like Presidio, Golden Gate Park, and Crissy Field to Ocean Park.
- Portland, Oregon, 220 plus miles of trails, home of the Nike Oregon Project, elite group coached by Alberto Salazar.
- Chicago, Illinois, with the flat Chicago Marathon, and trails like the Des Plaines River Trail.
- Boulder, Colorado, with Newton and Hoka based there, and many trails like Boulder Creek Path.
- Boston, Massachusetts, home of the oldest and most prestigious marathon and where distance running is a tradition.
- Eugene, Oregon, home of Track Town USA, where the late coach Bill Bowerman and the cofounder of Nike crafted shoes for his runners and with trails like the Amazon trail.
- And number one, New York, New York, with more than 50 running clubs and the New York Runners Association.

In Houston, many people converge in Memorial park early in the morning. Many groups put up tables along their routes with sags of water, fruit, and Oreo cookies. They mark their tables with their team names and respect to stop only in their own tables. Many running stores have organized runs. One that I find interesting is the Funky Fun Run in Fort Lauderdale Thursday evenings. The runners go out for three to five miles and end the run in the pool area of a hotel with fruit, drinks and a social time. In Miami and Fort Lauderdale the beach is transformed, the night with people going for dinner and walking around, later the people leaving the bars and parties walking with their drinks on hand, and then early in the morning hundreds of runners meet each other along the beach.

Weston Florida is a special place for sports. The way the city is laid out make it a very nice place to run. People meet in different parts crossed each other during the early morning run. If you want to meet a friend that you haven't seen in few days, just go out in the morning and run. It is like the Giro in Albania where the tradition is that around 6:00 pm people go out to walk along the main boulevard of the cities. If you want to meet somebody, just go to the Giro. If you are looking for something to do, just call a friend and tell her, "Hey I'll see you at the Giro." In Weston, we train on the roads, we go to the speed tracks, or we run hills in a manmade park with a hill that used to be a garbage fill. We have the First Monday of the month run, the Wednesday run with Weston Run Club, the Thursday run with Runners Depot, and the Saturday run with FIT or many of the other groups. We go to races, we have fun, we help each other, we build community, we motivate each other with healthy habits, we run our race, and we wait for others when they cross the finish line.

This Is My Race

You can run with friends, in teams or clubs. You can be running next to thousands of people, but at the end of the day, you are just running against yourself. You are running to compete with that voice that is telling you that it's too hard, asking yourself what you're doing here, or you should be at the beach. But there could be a voice that is telling you that you're going to hit a new PR, you're going to achieve a goal, you're supporting a cause, or you're going to honor a friend, a family, or a relative that is battling with cancer or cannot walk. You are running against yourself, because this is your race. When I look back at the race that God has traced for me, I can see that it has been designed in a unique way. There is no one in the whole world that has the same fingerprints you have, no one in the world has the same DNA that you have. In all the millions and millions of people of the world, you are made unique with a purpose that God has created for you. For me, it has been unveiled little by little and probably started to be revealed the day I was flying, rescuing people during the tragedy of Amero, Colombia.

Armero was a small town located at the valley just next to the big Volcano del Ruiz, covered by ice and snow. The day of the tragedy, the volcano started to release tons of volcanic ash, creating a big dark cloud. People in the town were confused, they didn't know what to do. Very few left the town, but the majority decided to stay since the ashes subdued. Unfortunately, during the night, while people were sleeping, massive pieces of ice broke loose from the cap of the volcano and melted. As it came down, it gained strength and pressure on the way down until it reached the bottom, erasing the whole town of Armero from the map. I remembered flying hours and hours in the helicopter taking people from the lake of mud. We heard reports on the news and on the radio about Omayra. One young girl got stuck under a pylon with only her head sticking out of the muddy water. The intent to get her loose failed and after days of listening to her on the radio, she died.

I saw families hugging each other laying on the mud and piles of debris of what was their homes. One of the most vivid moments was when we rescued a small boy wearing only pieces of a torn muddy t-shirt and pressing something with his hands. Later I saw that it was his belly and he was holding his guts that came out from a huge opening under his t shirt. The face of this little blonde boy was marked on my mind. I wondered what was going to happen to him with no family and in such conditions. The pain was too large to bear. After days of doing rescues from dawn to dusk, I went to sit on the mountain to look down on the camp. The helicopters were coming and going with victims that were treated. I prayed and said, "God if you have allowed me to be a pilot, I pray that from now on you use my skills to save people that need help" and my race began. You have to run to your destiny. it doesn't matter if you fail. You better try and fail then not try at all. Take the risk, even if the outcome is not what you expect. At least you took the risk. Run to your dreams, run to pursue happiness, to develop the talents that God gave you, and to cross the finish line.

I did many flights with the Colombian Air Force bringing doctors to remote places, and I felt inside that God was going to enlarge my territory. I saw an ad in an aviation magazine recruiting pilots for a mission aviation organization. I felt such a strong urge to keep that small ad and I put it in my wallet. Maybe five years later, my mom died. I felt like a piece of me was taken away, but at the same time I felt peace because my mom was going to be in a better place. I have such relief and thankfulness because in the last months of my mom's life, we talked about the promises of God and prayed together. I also felt like nothing was holding me, to let God do whatever he wanted to do with me. The images of the face of the little boy from Armero and the cry of Omayra kept coming to my mind. I remember the little ad that I put in my wallet years before, so I reached in and opened my wallet and the paper was still there. It was very old and torn. I could barely read the phone number, but come to find out it was a missionary organization that uses helicopters to bring hope to people in remote places of Africa, Asia and at that time, in Albania. To make the story short, one year later I was landing in Tirana, Albania, to be a missionary pilot for three years, bringing the love of God and humanitarian aid to people to the villages. That was part of my race. My race continued in Texas where I worked for more than ten years as an air ambulance pilot, and now, I am waiting to see what God is going to do with me the rest of the race. I just need to let him take me and direct me. It is like being in his hands. It is like putting my life in the hands of my father. It makes me think about a team of a father and son that ran marathons.

Maybe you are familiar with the story of Dick and Rick Hoyt. Rick is Dick's son, and when he was born, his umbilical cord was wrapped around his neck. It caused brain damage that confined him to a wheel chair for the rest of his life. He couldn't communicate normally. Rick was able to communicate using the computer developed by someone who used their talents to serve another. One day, he communicated to his father that he wanted to participate in a 5K benefit run that was organized in his neighborhood. His desire was to be in the race, and he asked his father to take him to the race. His desire was enough motivation for his father to go out and push him in his wheel chair during the race. When they finished the first race, Rick told his father that he felt freedom. He said that during that race he felt like if he could walk again, the feeling was very special and he wanted to do it again and that was the beginning of their race. They ran more than 100 marathons and many triathlons, and Dick did it all because Rick had a need. He had a dream. We all have dreams, and if we trust in our Heavenly Father, he can take us to places that we can't imagine, he can do what looks impossible, and will fulfill the desires of our heart if they agree to God's will for our life.

Dick put Rick in a small inflatable boat to pull him while swimming, then he carried him to a special seat that he made in front of the bike to ride with him, and finally he pushed him in the wheel chair to run with him. Many relate this story, to the story of a father's love. It really demanded from the father sacrifice, dedication, strength, and commitment to bring his son on those races. But I want to look at this story from Rick's perspective.

It was as much Rick's race as it was his father's race. He had to trust 100% in his father. He didn't know where the race was taking him. The water was rough sometimes, and if for some reason he got separated from his father, he would drift with no hope, not being able to swim, not being able to find his direction, and not being able to move the boat. He surrendered his life to his father and because he did that, he ran many races. I feel like Rick; the race is my race, but I depend 100% on my father, God, to take me to the places that he only knows, to bring me through the course, and to allow me to feel freedom, joy, and accomplish the impossible.

Maybe Rick was not able to see where he was going, maybe he couldn't see direction in his life. But his father showed to him little by little. If you find yourself in a place and time where there is no hope, where you don't see direction, trust in God. Surrender yourself to his direction and let him take you through the rough waters. He will show you little by little.

For Marcela, her race in life began also as a fulfillment of the God's plan for her life. Marcela is the director of FIT, and together with the great team of FIT, had touched the life of hundreds of people like me. She has helped them improve their lifestyle. FIT coaches, Brian, Cat, Christina, Denise, and Luis, together with their assistant coaches, offer a training program to help members achieve their goals of completing a half or full marathon. But it's more than a training program. FIT is a venue to help people become stronger, physically and mentally, and to create life-lasting relationships.

Marcela came to the USA in the late 80s and worked as a physical trainer when she was introduced to FIT. She was looking something other than the gym routine and heard about marathon training from a friend. She thought that it was not for her. She thought the training required for a marathon was training for elites and people that run fast. But her friend motivated her and she went to the training. It was a beautiful experience for Marcela. John Hall is the founder of FIT and he was Marcela's coach, something that Marcela learned from coach Hall was to "always keep moving forward". No matter what we are going through, even if seems that there is no hope, we need to keep moving forward. Marcela decided to start the training, but she didn't contemplate in doing a marathon. For her, it was something impossible, but she followed the program. When the time for the marathon came, Marcela was ready. She did her first half marathon in Tampa. She discovered a new passion and decided to train for the full marathon in Ottawa. When Marcela finished, there were no medals, no people around, even though everybody had finished. But her coach waited for her and give her his medal. She was determined to keep training for more races and not to let the circumstances unmotivated her.

FIT may have helped Marcela's character, but I would say God used FIT as a tool to help her character and her faith. Many of the things that Marcela and FIT does is by faith. The team, coaches, and assistant coaches are great people. Without them, FIT wouldn't be what it is. God uses people to help us in our life race; sometimes He puts us in situations where we must leave our ego aside and reach out to others to get help. And over everything, remember that God is on your side. Even if you feel like you are alone, you are the only one with your need. God is big enough to take care of that need, and many times he does it through people. The way FIT, the coaches, the assistant coaches, and the members touch the life of others is something that maybe can't be understood, but it's there. Maybe you think that you impact only a few people, but they impact others, and the others impact more people.

Something that FIT can offer is that is has a structure. When you want to achieve things in life, you need to develop a structure, a discipline. Many people come to FIT and they are not sure if they can do it. We tell them that many people have gone through FIT thinking the same, but they have followed the program, and they have made it. If doesn't matter the fitness level they have when they come to FIT; they are helped in order to develop what they need. Marcela has run already 75 marathons and the six world marathon majors. In one of those, the New York marathon she had the opportunity of wearing the colors of Colombia during the parade of nations. All the six majors are special, Tokyo with its parade, Boston with its legacy, and Berlin with the history. The impact that the wall made on Marcela was big, she thinks that sometimes we have walls in our lives that prevent us from doing many things.

In one of her races, Marcela was a pacer and was next to a lady from Detroit. After 8 miles, the flags, Achilles, and some others went ahead. Marcela stayed with Jackie, who left the snow to come down to Florida to participate in her first half marathon. She decided on that goal about a year ago and has been preparing dutifully for it. She had lost 40 pounds and the day of the race was the moment of truth! She started strong, but as the day got warmer, she slowed down, and it became a challenge for her. However, she was strong and determined, and Marcela was not going to let her give up on her dream. So, she stayed with her, encouraging her, and cheering her on. To make a long story short, they were the last half finishers at 4 hrs. and 19 minutes! She did it! They cried together at the end, and Marcela was very proud of her! And happy to be there to help her achieve her dream. They were the last ones, but they were victorious, they crossed the finish line, the price was a dream that came truth. Keep chasing your dreams, you can do it! Like Marcela, we can all make a difference in someone's life. Let's keep doing what we do. It's very simple.

Visualize Success

The idea is to run the race and to finish, is to be successful, but what is success? We need to define success. The Merriam Webster's definition of success is the favorable or desired outcome, also, the attainment of wealth, favor, or eminence (wealth, respect, fame), but this definition is outdated. Actually, there is a university that is trying to revise this definition in the dictionary. A survey sponsored by Strayer University (25) (Strayer Universisy, 2014) concluded that 90% of the 2,011 participants believed that success is more about happiness than power, possessions, or prestige, and 67% said they associate success with achieving personal goals; 66% defined success as having "good relationships with friends and family"; and 60% said it's about "loving what you do for a living." Only one of five mentioned monetary wealth. Dr. Michael Plater, president of Strayer University at the time of the survey said, "This indicates a clear change in the way Americans are thinking about their personal journey [their personal race]. It's no longer about the car or the house. Instead, people are focused on living a fulfilling life, whether that means finding a better career, achieving personal goals, or spending more time with their families." Success is love, honoring God, and knowing that you can't do everything alone. Each one of us has a goal, and success is to develop our talents and to live abundantly whatever is our passion and in doing that helping other people. This is independent of how much we have or our physical condition, a person with physical impediments can be very successful. Each person with their own personality and individuality is called for something, and when that is accomplished, there is success.

The habit of visualization is important because when you see what you want for your life, you are leading your life. When you visualize about your purpose and your mission in life, it will give you focus. Mel Robbins, a motivational speaker, television host, and CNN Commentator, talks about visualization (26) (Robbins, 2019) as a habit that you must have and is a powerful skill. Our brain has a system that allows certain information in, and blocks out other information. All this system is activated by is the healthy or unhealthy thoughts that we put in our mind. If we visualize ourselves and look into our lives with the best version of ourselves, we are going to see ourselves doing great things. Besides visualizing the things that we can have or do; we can visualize the positive emotions that we are going to have. It takes as little as 30 seconds to visualize yourself doing the skills that you want to have and the way that you want to be, so believe in yourself!

It is important to visualize success and what is success means for you. If there is a person that has a dream of writing a book, maybe some friends think it wasn't successful because he sold only 200 copies. But for him, it was a great success because he finished a dream and left a book for his children. He never even thought a certain number of copies, so for himself, he was very successful. I saw a movie about a triathlete In Spain called 100 Meters and was a true story. In the movie, he came last in the race. He came so late that everybody had left the race. Only his family and a handful of friends were waiting for him at the finish line. They were worried because most of the runners came in the late morning, but he came in the middle of night. Many could think that since he was last, that he wasn't successful, but that was the best day of his life, a great success, the culmination of years of preparation and more than that, the mark of the reunion of his family and the victory over a fight with multiple sclerosis. He lost his job because he was paralyzed for moments at a time, he struggled to find his identity in middle of doctors' visits, and had downturns from his sickness. When he went to the doctors' appointments, he saw people with no hope, almost ready to give up on life. He decided to be an inspiration for them, for himself, and his family. He started training for something he never did before: a triathlon. He trained for one year and found himself one morning on the beach paralyzed, not able to get out of the water. His coach and father-in-law pulled him out of the water. A coach that changed himself thanks to his inspiration, once an alcoholic, now somebody that could help him with his coaching talent. He recovered, but to do his triathlon, he needed to start all over again. He did it though with one more year of training. So, that night at the finish line, when he was the last runner, he accomplished the most wonderful race, trained two years for that race, fought with sickness, pain, frustrations, and losses but did it anyways. He crossed the finish line. He said, "If I only can run these 100 meters, then the next 100 will come and the next." But he was just taking small steps. For my friend Maria Beatriz, the 100 meters meant the same when she said if I only can run to that mailbox. And then the next will come, and then the next. The task may look too hard, or too big, but if we break it in parts, if we move from small goals to bigger goals, then it will be easier. The way to eat an elephant is one piece at a time.

For Marissa, the race is like life, there are up and downs, moments of happiness and moments when you feel tired. How to overcome difficulties is part of the race and is part of life, and for that, you need to gain strength. You need to train. So live your life the best you can. You need to gain strength in different areas, one of those is nutrition, you need to give your body what really needs.

The day of the race, fly your flight plan, don't try anything new, don't eat something that you haven't tried before. No new shoes, new shorts or a new shirt, no new socks. Try to bring your running gear in a carry-on with you and try not to check it in your luggage because if it gets lost and you have to buy new stuff, it's going to be bad. All these things should be tried in your long runs.

Start hydrating a few days before the race. Drink water before the race and during the race. Have a bathroom plan. Have a simple high carbohydrates breakfast; I like to eat oatmeal and eat fruit. Make sure you applied Vaseline or Body-Glide in the areas where chafing might occur. Have something to warm you up in before the race starts; maybe a sweater that you can throw away. I had already made the mistake of starting too fast a few times. Let your body warm up and pick up the pace. Make sure to drink along the route, even if it is cold or raining, you need to drink, your muscles need to be hydrated, otherwise you might have ended with cramps. Enjoy the race and draw energy from the cheer or from other runners. As for a nutrition plan, try to supplement every 45 minutes, or every 5 to 6 miles, with gels that are not heavy on the stomach. I personally like gels made with Chia seed, but now I am preparing my own gels. I mix certain nuts with organic protein powder, dates, raw cacao, coconut oil, coconut water, rice bran solubles, and turmeric, then I pack them in small zip lock bags. Thanks, Kristen, for the recipe; she is a great running and nutritional coach. For the long runs, you can set up few water spots or stash a sag maybe half way.

Try to mentally break the race in four parts and if you accomplish one of those parts and are getting down, lock your focus. Don't let your mind trick you. Be strong and courageous. Run the first 3/4 of the race with your mind, and the last 1/4 of the race with your heart! But may sure that even you have to crawl, cross the finish line.

If the mind is not synchronized with the body, surely you will not reach your goal.

Luis Tovar

Photo by Luis Tovar

All the work is done and I'm confident. I gave it all. Some days better than others but the commitment and passion was always the same. Time to focus on believing I can do it.

Ana Maria Villegas

Photo by Ana Maria Villegas

Think running is easy? If you've never trained 'til hurt. If you've never cried over an injury. If you've never crossed a finish line. You've never known running.

Friends in Training

Photo by Friends in Training

Chapter 5.

RUNNING WITH A PURPOSE

Purpose Starts with Gratitude

When I ran my first marathon in 2016, I enjoyed the whole race in Washington DC, but what left an impression in my life was at the Marine Corps Blue Mile. We gave a salute to our troops as a way to expresses gratitude to those that have given their life for our freedom. A mile with pictures of mostly young people that had laid their lives in the battle field was present at this spot. I have so much gratitude for this country, the country that gave me new opportunities, where my children were born and raised, where I have my home, my friends. It made me think about my values, gratitude, and determination. This country is a melting pot of cultures brought from immigrants and Native Americans with determination in hopes of building a better future. After the tragedy of September 11, 2001, I wanted to show that gratitude to the country so I joined the Navy Reserve. Running through the Blue Mile gave me the same feeling of thankfulness for those who died for us, especially when I saw mothers that were running, stop, and kneel in front of the pictures of their sons, tears running from their eyes mixing with their sweat. A light fog was covering the field, the only noise you could hear was the steps of the runners saluting the flags held by relatives of those who died for us.

It's the same gratitude that I feel for my country Colombia where I served in the Air Force. There were difficult times combating guerrillas and drug cartels, but at the same time, we gave a helping hand to people in need or distress. Many soldiers in Colombia, and also civilians in the conflict zones, gave their lives for the freedom of Colombians. Many were victims of land mines and lost their legs. There is a race in Colombia "Presta Tu Pierna" (loan your leg) (27) (Presta tu Pierna, 2019) to help those victims. Runners run with pants that have only one leg. It is a race with a purpose.

Ana Maria Villegas is the woman's winner of the 2018 Wings for Life race in Australia and the 2017 Wings for Life race in USA. In this peculiar race. you don't go to the finish line, but the finish line comes to you. The race takes place in 23 countries and starts at the same time. The World Run Wings for Life is one of the most fun races that I have been. Thirty minutes after the beginning of the race, a car starts chasing everybody, once the car passes you, then you finish. At that point, you go to the nearest pick-up point and a bus brings you to the start. It is kind of funny to finish a race in a bus, but that is the way it is.

Wings for Life is one of my favorite runs, if not my favorite. It is very special for me because it's where I met a person with a special place in my heart. We ran the first mile in Wings for Life 2016. Everything started when I saw her with her yellow, red and blue colors. It is special for me and for thousands of runners around the world. Exactly 120,054 runners participated in Wings for Life 2019. In the USA, there is only a flagship race in North America and it's in Sunrise Florida, five minutes from my house. In total, 323 locations in an event like the one in Sunrise or using an app with a virtual catching car. For us, it's our local international race. It is special for another friend, Madeline whose reflection on the 2019 World Run is, "For the three consecutive years of this race, I was proud of my records: 2014: 14.86 miles; 2015: 17.22 miles and 2016: 14.43 miles. This year-2019, I achieved a new PR (*peor* record): 10.79 miles; and yet, *I was elated*! Why was I so happy after performing so poorly on this race?

After much reflection I realized that for the last few weeks, I've been training in pain and discomfort in the Achilles tendon of my right leg, particularly during the 1-2 miles of exercise. I was deeply and unavoidably concerned. Unaware of whether I would have to reduce or even interrupt training runs, I continued to exercise/train with much caution and optimism. More importantly, I was concerned about the impact of this new persistent injury in my training for the Chicago marathon. Anyhow and for some strange reason, the pain has significantly subsided since yesterday afternoon soon after the end of the race. No signs of the pain when I left my bed this morning. This makes no logical sense (at least, not to me) and as some may classify it, it may be miraculous.

Geovanny, my husband, did not attend any of my previous three Wings for Life races. Yesterday, for the first time, he was not only attending but also participating in the race. I told myself that I had to do everything in my power to make this a memorable and pleasant experience for him. Unlike most participating in this event, Geo hates running. Normally, on long runs, I run further and faster than him. Yesterday, on the other hand, I planned to run alongside him. I wanted to experience the rush of being chased by the "catching car" with him by my side. The look on his face as we tried to prevent the unavoidable was going to be priceless. Well, that never happened. Geo left me in the dust soon after we crossed the 8-mile marker. He was running this race because I begged him – not expecting to run more than 6-8 miles and now, he was exceeding his performance expectations in much comfort. I was not happy, I was thrilled!

During my 9+ years of competitive running, I've ran many races in which I've encountered and met many wonderful and talented individuals. To this day, some of these runners are considered my friends. With many of them, I've continued to train and enjoy life experiences outside of the running world. Furthermore, some have become our chosen family members. Wings for life 2019 was special! I was able to run alongside runners I deeply respect and admire; many of them ran pass me but cared enough to shout a motivational word or phrase as they did. These are runners who inspire me each and every day for their dedication and discipline. They are the ones who prevent me from throwing the towel and retiring from the sport. To all of those runners: THANK YOU for having such an effect in my spirit and my soul! I am forever grateful for your unconditional love and support!

Wings for Life is the only race where so many runners from so many different countries run at the same time and for a common cause: research of spinal cord injuries. We run for those who can't! As I ran yesterday, I thanked God for the opportunity to do something I truly enjoy in good health and in the company of my husband and so many beautiful souls and talented individuals that I call my wonderful friends!"

This huge race, sponsored by Red Bull, has a purpose – it is to help spinal cord research. It is to bring hope to somebody that doesn't have the facility of walking or running like we do. We need to be thankful because we can run, we can move. But let's don't forget those that can't run, that can't move, and don't have what we have. There is a purpose for Wings for Life, there is a purpose for everything. My question for you is, what is your purpose?

Our purpose doesn't mean to do things for free to other people. It means to put our talents for the service of others. It means to develop our gifts. The benefit is either monetary or just self-fulfillment will come. Success means to unlink the result from the action; the real reward is in doing it, not in the result.

Our Race in Life

In the little town of Trogen, Switzerland, one of the people that I admire the most was running with a group of friends and supporters to celebrate the anniversary of Helimission. The run took them through green pastures of rolling hills of the Swiss prairie, where beautiful flower beds decorated the windows of picturesque traditional houses, brown cows were laying in the fields and neighbors greeting each other. African choirs and Swiss yodeling were waiting at the finish line; this was the home of Helimission. His name is Ernie Tanner and he has one of the most interesting races in life. His race started when he gave his life to the Lord when he was watching the news of the Vietnam war and saw how helicopters rescued the injured. God gave him the vision of using helicopters as a tool to reach the unreachable, to offer humanitarian aid in places so remote that would take days, weeks, or months for help to arrive. Ernie sold his house and purchased a helicopter to go to Cameroon and help missionaries with their work. In that helicopter, he learned to fly and with only around 25 hours of flight time, he started the journey of his solo flight from Switzerland to Cameroon.

Just few minutes into the flight to Cameroon, he had to land in a farm. I can't imagine the look of the owner of the house when he saw a helicopter landing in his yard and a young pilot get out to ask for directions. That was only the beginning of the trip that took Ernie through the Sahara Desert with no GPS or airports along the route to refuel. Ernie had to trust people. The day before the flight, he met a person that drove a truck carrying his fuel at some point along the way in the middle of the dessert. That person could easily run with his money or not being in the right place at the right time, but Ernie trusted in him and in God to bring him to the other side. Now, Helimission has bases in different countries with families that left a comfortable life to respond to the call that God has placed in their lives, and to run their races. Some of the countries where Helimission has brought his helping wings are Chile, Cameroon, Kenya, Ethiopia, Madagascar, Indonesia, Papua Guinea and Albania.

Like Ernie, we all are born with a purpose in our lives. God knew us from before we were born, formed us in the womb of our mothers, and made our DNA. In my life I have been involved in few accidents that could easily result in something more serious than what happened. I was involved in an accident with my sister and my aunt that turned the car upside down. We were spinning in the middle of an expressway, and when we stopped, we crawled out of the car that was smashed without a single scratch. On another occasion, I was ejected from a car when the driver, my friend, couldn't gain control on a wet road after a hard break to avoid hitting a dog that crossed in front of us. I start rolling downhill of a mountain, and when I stopped few hundred meters down, I got up without a single scratch. Another time, when I was 15, I was hit by a bus and taken to a hospital where I was pronounced dead. I woke up hours later with without a single scratch. I was involved in many military operations with grenades exploding near our landing zone, bullets crossing all over the place, and not a single scratch. All of these experiences I made out alive because God was protecting my life. He created me with a purpose and he was protecting me so I could accomplish that purpose. Not all stories are the same, though. My cousin Robert's daughter died around the age of ten because of cancer, but I know we will see her again. Even in that short life, she accomplished her purpose. We might think God is not fair and wonder why things happen that way. Our life is just a little snapshot of eternity, and we were created with a purpose for the little time we spend on earth.

Maria Beatriz is another beautiful story of how she found purpose in life and in running. She came to the USA about 9 years ago, coming from a normal routine where things were uneventful and not much exercise involved. Exercise was spontaneous, classical yo-yo, with ups and downs. When she saw her dad and mom and sister doing sports, she felt like it would be something nice for her, but at the same time impossible. The unbalance that came from being in a new country resulted in some extra pounds. When her first son was born, new challenges were placed on her life. Her son's special therapy, and handling schedules were stressful, thus her first feelings anxiety were experienced. I identified with her when she said that she felt something like an unexplainable fear, or uneasiness overcome her. Things change when her sister Monica, a marathoner, invited her to run. Her answer was, "That's not for me, but I'll try." She literally started from scratch. She started an eight-week plan, but really, everything started in her mind when she put her running shoes on, opened the door, and took the first step towards a new life full of faith and determination.

The approach that Mariabe took was like doing homework; she couldn't go to bed at night without doing her homework. She started doing walk-run-walk intervals and put markers on a mailbox to start. She probably thought by the next mailbox she was going to die, but if she survived, she'll try to make it to the next mailbox. And that day in her first 30 minutes of running, she discovered that she could accomplish a challenge. She didn't die, so she decided to do it the next day, and the next day, and the next. It became a discipline and a commitment. Now, Mariabe helps many achieve the same goals that she has by sharing her story; that made her accountable. That make the days become weeks, and the weeks months. The motivation was the idea of competing with herself, the idea of becoming better and better; Kaizen! The improvement went from running one-minute and walking one minute, to running straight for 5 minutes, 10 minutes, then 15 minutes. When she run 20 minutes straight for the first time, she cried. It was the switch in her mind, the certainty of yes, she can do this. She believed in herself and the impossible was no longer there. She was ready for her first 5K. But before, she did a practice run with a time of 45 minutes that she never will forget, and then the Color Run with a time of 38 minutes. She took a photo of her shoes and said, "Finally I found something that make me feel happy!"

She was getting ready to do a race, and boom! She was pregnant again. More changes and new challenges. She had to stop running for a while and the stress started creeping in again. She remembered when she ran and how she felt good and said, "I always want to feel this way, I always want to feel good." And she started training again. She imposed upon herself the discipline of training. The only difference this time is that she did it more for obligation than for enjoyment, so she stopped running. It's like our relationship with God; the moment we start a relationship based on formalities and obligations; we stop doing something that is fun. My desire of being in the presence of God is because it's something that I enjoy and that I seek, not something that is imposed on me.

For some time Mariabe, didn't feel very well. She started running again slowly, increasing little by little. This time, the change was from doing homework in taking medicine, and with God's help, this brought new energy to Mariabe. She became a 100% runner. She sees running as a tool for mental health. With all the things that need to be done a home with the children, with work, or the house, it's hard to adjust. It is harder to commit than to make the space to adjust the schedule. But she chose the commitment. The time that she spent running became a nonnegotiable part of her life. At the beginning, she had to deal with the anxiety and when she went running, she saw anxiety and fear like spectators with ugly faces behind of the fence, looking at her with the intentions of reaching her but detained by the fence. She started thinking that she was in control and that those fears and anxiety never could catch her. They always were there, but she was in absolute control of everything around her. Running helped her because running depends only on you. She started slowly with one 5k, then another. The visits to her therapist became less frequent and then came her first 10k. Now, she runs three days a week and combines exercise with yoga or spinning.

In this process, Mariabe realized she had a mission in her life. She wanted to be who she really is, and that comes together in her purpose in life. It's part of her identity, so she started working towards developing that purpose. Everything in life requires work and preparation. Running a marathon requires work and preparation. For her, the day began when she shared her experience with people in same circumstances. After one year, she saw herself not like she was before; on the mirror, she saw a much better person. Mariabe was thankful to God for what she lived. She started sharing all her exercises and tips in her social page. Many people came to her, and she felt that if she could help somebody feel better and go through the difficulties of their life, she would be the happiest person in the world. That was her mission in life and there was nothing to stop her from finding a way to carry on with her mission. She started thinking for a name for her dream, and realized that when she went running, she came back a happier mom. Thus, she called it "Happy Run, Happy Mom". It's an organization that helps moms to deal with their stress, fears, and anxieties. She shares tips with a focus on personal development and using running as a tool to have a healthier body and mind. She is not a professional coach; she just shares her heart. This year, she started a challenge called Happy 100 Days Moving where people are committed to move and exercise, even if it is just walking for 30 minutes every day, for 100 days. It has been a great success; many moms have started to run and leaving a sedentary life style. Every 100 days is a new edition, now she is in the third edition. The group get together to run on Saturdays besides their own routines on weekdays. They motivate each other and keep track of the progress and give feedback on their own experiences and how they have managed to keep up with their activities and still making time for exercise.

Mariabe has become a blessing. She has had always a positive support from her friends, mainly from her sister Monica and her mom, a person that despite adversities, has always had a positive outlook of things. Now, she is the support of many others. She had many trials that have made her message a reality and made her the best version of herself.

The race is the result of the preparation. It is the celebration. A medal means something different for everybody, but everybody wins when they accomplish something they have proposed to do. In life, we also need preparation, consistency, trial, and error. Many times, you will have desire and motivation and sometimes you will do it only because you know is something you must do. You will face obstacles, but you must do it. We need to have joy when we go through trials, knowing that the test of our faith produces patience and character.

Nothing is Too Small

When I heard that my children are volunteering for activities like helping cleaning school rooms during summer break, or packing food and clothes to send to Venezuela, or giving water at a race, I felt very proud and happy to see that they are giving something away for others. We can find a purpose in our life, but when it involves doing something for somebody else, it's really a greater purpose; it is running the real race, and you can run with purpose. It can be something as small as entering a race that gives the proceeds to an organization. For example, Wings for Life gives 100% of the entries to spinal cord research. Or, it can be raising funds for a charity or helping somebody to complete his race.

Many of my dearest friends are from Venezuela. Right now, the country is going through a very bad situation; a country that once was prosperous is at the border of collapse and many have opted for leaving. Right now, more than 50,000 people are crossing the border into Colombia daily at one single point. The exodus brings these people through the border walking with their suitcases and heading to other cities of Colombia, Ecuador, Peru. They must cross the high mountains in the middle of hard weather conditions and cross the paramo to make their way to Bogota. Many others from Venezuela are settling in cities around the world like Madrid, Miami, and Mexico. Many of them do random jobs and you may think is not their race, but things happen and the least we can do is help, even with something little.

Sometimes I get a text from my friend Salvador saying that he got some pastries for free and asking if we can bring them to the homeless. Or I'll get a text from my friend Jose or Mariela to collect medications, clothes, or food to send to Venezuela. My friend Patty collected aid to send to Puerto Rico after the hurricane that hit the island. Our help can be something big or something small; even giving a tip, a smile, a visit to a sick friend, sending a note of encouragement, basically anything that takes the eyes away from yourself to do something for somebody else is a blessing. Every time you do something for somebody, you are making one more step of your race. For those suffering or going through difficult times, it's hard to think that they are running their race. It feels more like they are stuck. But with faith and the belief that we can trust God and that there is a calm after the storm, we can do best we can do in whatever we do by helping each other.

What We See Started with Is What We Don't See

Everything starts with a dream. Everything that is in the realm of what we see, happened before in the realm of what we don't see. The chair that you are sitting on, the building where you are in, anything. Before something happens, one person thinks about it, designs it, draws it, and then it happens. The marathon of New York, for instance, is the product of one man's dream. It's the biggest of all the marathons, in numbers at least. My third world major was the New York Marathon.

The marathon crosses the five Boroughs of NYC. Everything started when a man from Romania named Fred Lebow had the idea of organizing a race of four loops around Central Park. The first New York Marathon was in 1970, had 55 finishers, and has grown to have more than 50,000 finishers in 2018. People from more than 80 countries come to the race. For Fred Lebow, his real race was the race itself. He was involved in the garment industry, but his purpose in life was with organized running; it was to produce another of the icons of New York. Fred found running like an oasis in his life. Central Park was his inspiration, but he wanted to bring the race to the Bronx and the other Boroughs. He wanted to bring the world to the race and expand his horizons. It is the same idea of advancing or doing something better and something bigger. It is like the prayer of Jabez where Jabez asks God to bless Him and enlarge his territory. That is in God's heart to enlarge our territory, our circle of influence, our performance, and our legacy. The entry fee for the first race was about 50 cents to a dollar, and there were less spectators than runners. Fred's crazy ideas like "Three Crazy Legs Mini Marathon" to promote the race among women helped launch the race to a higher level. The Gal Mini Marathon of 6 miles attracted over 1,000 participants and was a complete success. Fred's circle became the New York Runners Club and was almost like a fraternity.

Fred worked very hard and wouldn't have made what he did if it wasn't for the help of the volunteers that put hard and long hours of work. By 1975, Central Park was no longer suitable for the marathon; the amount of people was so big that judges were not able to keep up with who was who and how many miles everyone was completing. The Boston Marathon became the inspiration to take the NYC marathon to the roads. The goal was to celebrate the 1976 Bicentennial by taking the marathon to the Boroughs. The financial condition of New York was in bad shape and created an environment of tension and crime in the Bronx, as well as other areas of the city. The idea of running a marathon through those areas was considered very dangerous and risky, almost like running for your life. But the event became giant. The New York Runners Club didn't have the money or the runners that Fred assured the media they had, so he went and found sponsors and invited elite runners to attract more people. Fred was brilliant in getting people to become involved and made them feel like the race belonged to them. Kids of the hood, almost like gangsters, were persuaded by Fred to become marshals of the race. Two thousand participants came to the first race through the five Boroughs in 1976. The race was a success and Bill Rodgers took first place. The people from Harlem changed hostility for hogs. The race coincided with the rebirth of the city and brought running to the footsteps of many in America. Fred was flying in his race, his real race, and the purpose of his life. He brought unity, peace, and harmony to the five boroughs of New York. The numbers doubled year by year when international runners started coming. Other big cities followed New York, like London and Chicago, where they opened the door for road running. Fred Lebow ran about 68 marathons, but not the one he organized, for being so busy coordinating the NYC marathon he could never run it. In 1992, he celebrated his 60th birthday running the NY marathon for first time after being diagnosed with brain cancer. He died in 1994, but he accomplished his dream, he ran his race, and he crossed the finish line.

Pass the Blessing

One of the great purposes that we have in life is to pass on our blessings. We should be like a river that takes water from one side and let it run through to pour water on the other side. God has created us that way; we don't want to be like a tank that takes water from one side and doesn't let any water come out. The stagnation will cause the water to become nasty. If somebody has helped me, it's so I can help somebody in return. When I started to run, many people like Christina, Marcela, and Coach Luis helped me get better. But now was my time to help, even if that meat sharing the little that I knew. When I started studying the Maffetone Method, some people came to me asking what I was doing that made improved my running so much. I learned good things from Dr. Maffetone and Coach Luis, and I wanted to share that. We started a little group to put it in practice together. It was so nice to see people improve. My great and beautiful friend Luisa, for example, made so much progress that people noticed how well she was running. The best part was not really her improvement, but the fact that when I was gone for few months, Luisa took people under her wing to pass along what she learned. The student became better than the teacher. She has such heart for people and I enjoy seeing how the blessing pass from one hand to another. We are better in life if we find a mentor for us and if we find a protégée, or somebody to take from and somebody to give to. It is so simple, yet so rewarding. It is good to inspire others. I remember when I went to work in Houston for two months, I talked to a girl about running and she told me, "You inspire me. I am going to start running" and she did. I want to inspire you to maybe to write a book, start a blog, to share your faith to motivate others, to start running, or to start something different.

Passing blessings can happen in any moment of our day. It can be something simple for us but of huge impact for others. When Marcela runs as pacer, she keeps in mind that she can make a difference on others. During the West Palm Beach Marathon 2018, she had the most emotional race as a half Marathon sweeper. She started with about 12 walkers where about six of them on a team carrying the American Flag. Others were from Achilles and other ladies on their weight loss journey. Achilles itself is an organization with purpose. They empower people with physical disabilities to accomplish their personal achievements in running events. The program focusses on running, but running is just a simple tool to bring hope, inspiration, and joy in achievement.

We need to live in a simple world and make things simple. Things need to flow. If there is too much frustration and stress, maybe it's not the right time and maybe it's not meant to be. Yes, we need to be persistent, we need to fight, but we need to leave the burden. We need to rest and that is why I love the Lord. He takes my burdens, he gives me rest in the middle of the fight, the hassle, and the grinding. We need to make things simple and listen to our intuition. In running we say, "Listen to your body. If your body is telling you that you are overtraining, maybe it's because that is happening. If it's telling you feel heavy and lazy, it's maybe because you can push more. If something doesn't feel right maybe it's because something is going on that you don't know about." My life is very simple, all I do is enjoy time with my kids, enjoy time with my friends, and enjoy time with the Lord. All I need is a pair of running shoes to go out and exercise, eat healthy, go to work, and that's it. I enjoy a sunrise, a full moon, a conversation, a book, writing, and running. I don't need to go to expensive luxurious places to have fun; I just enjoy the here and now. We need to be content and not put our happiness in material things. Sure, if we get to go to a luxurious place, do extraordinary things, or have uncommon moments; we enjoy those things. But either simple or luxurious, it's the same. If we live on purpose, we can enjoy life either way. Life doesn't need to be hard. If we make our life easy, we can thrive, we can develop our full potential, and we can express ourselves. We can choose between making things simple or to complicate things. We need to have the faith of a child. Children are spontaneous since they know their parents are caring for them. We need our inner child to come out, stop being so tense and anxious, and leave the stress on the pavement. We need to see the glass half-full and not half-empty. I learn from my past, have vision on my future, but live in the present. How do we know if tomorrow we will be alive? We should live this day as if it's our last day. If I want to be loved, then I need to love. If I want to be blessed, then I need to bless. I live day-by-day, and what I sow, I will reap.

In his inaugural speech, President Kennedy said, "Ask not what your country can do for you, ask what you can do for your country." I would like to take that idea and say it's not what others can do for you, but what you can do for others. Whatever you sow you reap. In Berlin, I got the privilege of running next to Judge Craig Mitchell. He is a live example of the power of encouragement. Judge Mitchell went to Berlin, not only to run the marathon with some of the people he helped, but to tell his story which is the inspiration for the movie Skidrow Marathon. He was frustrated because he used to sentence people. But then he asked himself what he could do to bring light of hope in dealing with the root cause of bad decisions that turned into bad actions and ended in his court.

One of the defendants whom Judge Mitchell sentenced to prison approached him after his release. He asked the Judge to visit him at the Midnight Mission Homeless Shelter where he was living. After the visit, the judge decided to start a running club. He thought that if he could get few of these men and women into shape and run marathons, the benefits would cross over into their personal lives. He promised those who stick with the program and stay clean a free trip to run in an international marathon.

Judge Mitchell suffers from a painful spinal condition and has been told by his doctors to stop running. He found a purpose that is bigger than his pain. He started the running club and this gives him the opportunity to change the world in a way that he can't do in his own courtroom. This peculiar running club do their long runs in the middle of the one of the most dangerous areas of Los Angeles. When they go out to run, they see tents of homeless people and drug dealers living on the street. They cross streets with maybe a pair of shoes hanging from the power lines, or other kind of mark showing that they have entered the territory of a dangerous gang. The risk created tension, but with time, people got to know them and what they want to accomplish. They let them go by unharmed.

The runs started at the Midnight Mission where people who were almost forced to attend the trainings now look at the training as the highlight of the week. One of the members touched by Judge Mitchell is an amazing musician and was once a professional who played bass guitar in a heavy metal band. Unfortunately, he failed his race when alcohol and drugs destroyed his career. But it didn't destroy his life. After losing everything, he also lost hope. Yet, Judge Mitchell gave him a hand. He joined the running club weighing nearly

300 lbs. with nothing to lose and only a dream in his pocket, studying music and film at the San Francisco Conservatory of Music.

Another runner is a girl that struggled to find a second chance with her infant son. She moved to LA to start a new life, but drugs and drinking kept being that wall that she couldn't pass. She ended at the Midnight Mission Family Shelter where she found that second chance. I would say it's where God met her with that new hope. Her criminal history had marked her with scars and people were hesitant in giving her the chance that she needed. People fail, but our God is a God of second chances. Any criminal story can be forgiven by Him, and with Him, our life can be new. God can make a way where there is no way.

Judge Mitchell followed his heart to accomplish his purpose. With two things in his personal inventory, his desire to help people and his legs, Judge Mitchell was able to pass the blessing. Maybe we are not perfect, maybe we don't have millions or are famous, but we have something. Whatever that is, it's that something can become a blessing.

Stay Hydrated

When we go to races, we have to stay hydrated. We found water every mile. Volunteers get up early in the morning so they could do something better. They decide to drive to the place, spend their own gas, pay their own parking, and lift boxes, bottles, and jars to provide water to the runners. We take the cup, pour the water on our head, drink it, and stay strong. The most revolutionary invention of all time is the aqueduct. You go to several places in your house and open a valve, and boom! The precious liquid runs through. You can drink it, you can cook with it, and you can wash with it. In places like La Guajira, Colombia, things work a little bit different. If there is a river close by, you take two five gallons jars and walk hours to the river. You fill the jars and bring them home to boil the water. Still many particles stay in the water. Some of the Wayuu people don't have a river close by, so the system is different. They open a hole on the ground, spend many hours or days digging out the dirt, and then wait. When the rain comes, the holes are filled, and that is where they get their water from.

La Guajira in Colombia is a peninsula in the Northern part of the country and is shared with Venezuela. The emerald blue water of the Caribbean Sea surrounds this vast desert. The children of the Wayuu live there in small settlements called rancherias. From a distant, they could see the wind blowing and the image of somebody riding a bicycle coming their way. What initially was a mirage, turned into a woman dressed in local fashion. Her dress blew like a flag as she moved the pedals with great effort. The tires of the bike were bigger than normal to get traction on the sand, it was a beach bike with more effort and less speed. As she got closer, the children recognized the sun-tanned face of Alexandra pulling a small trailer with some books with her. They welcomed Alexandra with some water to quench her thirst after her long journey of 20 miles. After a little break, Alexandra greeted the group of children and started teaching and reading to them. Before she left, she took the books that she left the week before and replaced them for the ones that she brought with her. She was ready to take those to another rancheria.

The Wayuu people has been affected by the actual crisis in Venezuela; the border is closed, there is not commerce, and children and old have malnutrition. For the Wayuu, the main success is in their death. Their wealth is in their land and their cattle. A funeral can take up to one month of celebration. They celebrate their death because is the finish line. When someone dies, many people from other rancherias come to be with the family and to celebrate the race that they have finished. They have many traditions, but now they have new dreams that they have found through the education and books.

The first time Alexandra came to La Guajira was with her family. They moved there from their hometown in Bogota because Alexandra's husband accepted a job as an engineer. After finishing his contract with that company, uncertainty came to the future but he had a response from a very good international company. They were getting ready to start a new journey one day when the family was eating dinner. But Alexandra's husband started coughing blood. The cancer that spread in matters of months took his life. Now, as a widow, Alexandra decided to do what she and her children wanted to do: go back and continue her race. Not knowing how, she began bringing books that she had accumulated from her work in the schools in Bogota.

With small steps, she started with few books to reach one family, and then more kids and more books. People found the way to help and to put in their small contribution. A radio station knew about Alexandra's work and started a campaign to collect books across nation. Books pour out, just as the water pours out. It was a small contribution, a few laps, and a few dollars. But each small contribution was a part of something that worked mysteriously to affect lives of people that I don't even know, like the life of one of Cesar's friends. Cesar is Alexandra's son and his friend learned a lot through the work of Alexandra. Now, he is going to the university and has entered, with Cesar, into a competition for social youth entrepreneurship in Colombia.

Well, my purpose is to help as much people as I can. It happens that I met a group of engineers in Texas that invented a filter that can filter any kind of water and mud, even if it has waste, animal feces, or some other type of contamination. It can be filtered to produce 100% clean potable water. Now I have four things in my inventory: my purpose, a desire to help people, a knowledge of where to get these kinds of filters, and my legs. What can I do with these tools? I decided to organize "Running for Hope", a race where our friends go and run loops in a park. For each loop, they donate money to purchase filters. We sent filters to La Guajira, Colombia last year and this year we are doing the same. This time, we are going to send filters to Guatemala. So, let's all together come to help. We can run, donate, and deliver filters that can provide clean water for a family.

There are so many things to do. There is almost one 5k race for any contribution for many different causes. People that have seen their inventory and have asked, "What can I do with what I've got?" For all you runners or walkers, that have volunteered in some fashion, that have gone and run the race to support the cause, I want to say thank you. Thank you on behalf of all those people that you have touched with your generosity.

Photo by Luis Tovar

Your goals can be accomplished by yourself but is better if you do it with the help of others.

Once you face the moment when you want to stop, be ready to dig deep inside of your heart to search for that spark of energy to help you ignore the pain.

Ana Maria Villegas

Photo by Ana Maria Villegas

Photo by Luis Tovar

Chapter 6.
NO EXCUSES

There are No Limitations

I have so much admiration for Nick Vujicic. He is a man with a wonderful family, two children, and his beautiful wife. He is a happy man that goes around the world bringing the message of hope and faith. Nick swims many laps during the week, as it is an exercise that keeps him strong and energized. But it wasn't always like that for Nick. When he was 8 years old, he was depressed. At 10 years, he tried to commit suicide by drowning himself. All of this was because he felt different. And he is. He is different because he has no limbs. In one of his conferences, Nick asked three questions to his audience, number one, who are you and what are your values? Number two, what is your purpose here in life? Number three, what is your destiny when you are done here? And then he said, if you don't know the answer to those questions, you are more disabled than me.

The story of Nick is a miracle. It was a birth difficult to cope for his parents. He was bullied and his low self-esteem brought him to the point of suicide. But later, he became the school captain, obtained a double degree, and got an amazing job. How did he do it? Nick is Australian born and has climbed over any obstacle imaginable with no arms and no legs. Every obstacle became an opportunity. That is the way we need to face problems: problems are not problems, they are opportunities. Like Nick likes to say, "No arms, no legs, no worries mate." If he starts feeling sorry about himself, he knows that he is focusing on something that he shouldn't. So, he renews his mind. The definition of disabled, for Nick, is a person that is not able to do anything. But Nick is somebody that has been able of doing more than any at his age, with more merit because he must approach life in a different way, like playing golf, or driving a car. The love for life and enthusiasm of Nick is contagious. Nick has one small foot that propels him when he is swimming. It allows him to drive, to steer a boat, to eat, and to write. He is thankful for his little foot, he is thankful for what his has. He preaches in churches and gives inspirational talks to people around the world and tells them that no matter where you are, what you have done, who you are, or what you have gone through, God knows it. He is with you and he is going to pull you through.

God is on your side. I know this personally. I remember when I came to Florida 28 years ago, I was driving a taxi, and had to spend long hours in the car to make some descent money. I didn't have friends. I didn't talk to anybody for weeks, except for normal talk to get things done. But never a single conversation with anybody. I sat at tables to eat by myself month after month, year after year. I came to a point of loneliness and depression, and I couldn't take it anymore. One night, I was so desperate that I start screaming in the car at the top of my lungs, "God help me, I need to know people!" At that very moment, I saw a billboard sign on the road that said, "God is on your side." I felt peace and I felt his presence. I didn't feel alone. One year later, I had many friends. The funny thing is that I drove the next night to the same place and the sign was gone. I had many friends, but what is more important is that I have God on my side, and he has given me dreams.

I believe God can bring new things to our life, but we need to facilitate those things with our determination. Our determinations will bring a consequence, and determination needs effort. For me, effort is doing all that I possible can in my strength to accomplish something and to leave all that is beyond my strength in God's hands. I finished the Chicago Marathon in 3:51 with my personal record, it was my PR. For the last runner it was also his personal record. Probably over 9 hours, we both were winners, although for him the finish was more exciting. When Maickel Melamed crossed the finish line, he was surrounded by people with flags, mainly from Venezuela – his home country. He was on the news and his muscular dystrophy was no excuse for him to not accomplish his dream. His message was, "I gave it all, I lived it all and that is my desired for everyone, give it all, lived it all."

Too Young

FIT has a group that meets at the speed track, FIT kids. It's full of children from 4 to 12 years old who come to practice and learn under the leadership of Marcela, Audrey, and Veronica. There is an assistant coach that is very special, his name is Adrian Gandara. He is an 11-year-old boy who started running when he was four. Adrian helps other kids run better and also trains them in stretching. When Adrian tried to learn to ride a bike with the training wheels, he didn't like it very much. He asked his dad if he could run instead, but his father told him no. He wanted to see him riding the bike. Adrian persisted though, and kept asking day after day if he could run. After more than one month asking, his father said yes. He ran about three miles next to his dad who was riding the bike. Adrian was persistent with his father. We need to be persistent. If we ask God, and keep on asking God, he will give you the desires of your heart according to his will. And of course, he is not going to give you something that is harmful to you or others.

Coming back to Adrian's story, Adrian not only started running, he did exercises to improve his technique and endurance. When he was seven, he did his first race. He got first place for his age and that motivated him to keep going. He kept winning, and at the age of 11, he has completed around 120 races. His longest race was the A1A half-marathon in Ft. Lauderdale with a time of 1:46. Adrian has such joy for running that he motivated his dad, mom, and brother to run, and now sometimes they go running as a family. Two of his favorite races were a 5K that he did in 22:14 minutes, an amazing time considering that it was a trail on grass and dirt, and more amazingly, he got the world record for his age. The second was another 5K in 20:6, and again took the world record from somebody that took it from him one month after his first record race. Adrian's biggest dream at the moment is to go to the Footlocker Race in 2024, the greatest race for high schoolers, and then the Olympics in 2028. Adrian is focused and has a vision already. There is no excuse. Adrian wants to keep running until his body tells no more, maybe 100 years.

Joanny Rodriguez came to USA at the age of 11. She started playing soccer, but she got a meniscus tear. To recover, she started running. She signed up for a 5K and she finished in 45 min. She didn't have the proper training, but when she crossed the finish line, she knew that running was what she wanted to do from now on. She started training for the Miami Marathon. One time when she was doing speed training in the track, she was observed by the Venezuelan team coach. She went to Venezuela with him for the team trials and was included in the national team. She trained in Florida and later was sent by the team to train in California; she was on the team for about five years. She was sent to Texas to train with great national coaches like Bill Collins and Isaac Murphy to prepare for the Olympic trials for Rio. She had a time of 11.02 sec in the 100 meters, but unfortunately lost the last trial for 0.4 seconds and couldn't make it to Rio. She kept going anyways. Later on, Joanny decided to switch from spring running to distance running. Now, Joanny runs ultramarathons; she went from one extreme to other, from 100 meters to 100 miles. She became a sport therapist and running technique coach.

Too Old

There is a runner in Argentina, her name is Elisa Forti. She is 82 years old and has ran the "Crossing of the Andes", a 100-kilometers, three-day race from Chile to Argentina, more than 5 times. Her mom was 107 years old. Before she died, she told her, "How are you going to do the race? Be careful." Elisa said, "I don't know if I am going to finish, all I know is that I am going to start." In life, things don't happen unless you take the first step. That is called faith. You see, you don't know where God is going to take you unless you are in motion. It's like you are on a horse, unless you make the first step and put the horse in motion, you won't be able to steer it. You need faith, so jump and take the first step. A cruise ship is a huge boat, but unless is in motion it won't be able to turn. God wants to turn our lives, but we need to be in motion. We need to take the risk, make the move, pop the question, go in front of the microphone, let go of the brake, make the cut, put the brush on the canvas, sign the contract, and play the cord. We need to make the move.

Every time I see 73-year-old Jose Yamamoto in a race, I see him wearing emblems of Peru, his home country, on his shirt. He started running about 14 years ago when he was 59. He did the first half-marathon in 2006 and from there has complete around 125 half-marathons and 41 full marathons. He runs five days a week and combines races with exercise. Before he started running, his physical activity was minimal, and once in a while he would go to the gym. When his son suggested him to start running, he thought it was a crazy idea because he barely walked.

From almost no activity to walking, to jogging, to running, Jose didn't let his age be in the way to becoming a great marathoner. He says, "If I start something, I am going to finish it." Determination and consistency are his mottos. He made many changes in his discipline and his nutrition. He eliminated all processed food and paid attention to proteins, iron, and carbohydrates.

Jose has a friend that had an incorrect medical treatment that resulted in a stroke while he was running. When friends that were running with him saw him having the stroke, they acted quick. They stopped running and called 911 and opportune assistance came. During his recovery time, Jose and his group kept giving him encouragement. His friend, with a strong will, came back to running, but this with the help of Jose and his group. The friends that Jose has met while running had become like brothers; They are my heroes. Actually, many know his group as the superheroes, because they dress up like superheroes. They travel nationally and internationally. There is Batman, Superman, Captain America, Ironman, the Oak of the Asphalt, Supergirl, Flash Girl, and the beautiful Peruvian Thunder. These heroes don't fly nor have supernatural powers, but they are my superheroes. They have determination and commitment and are there for their loved ones. I am not writing stories about superstars, people that live in their own world, spending half of their lives to make themselves known, and the other half to hide from the public and the paparazzi. I am writing stories about superheroes that are normal people, like you and me, who keep grinding every day, because the grind never stops. I write of superheroes because they have given something from themselves to affect the life of others. Normal people that have suffered the down turns in life and had risen to new beginnings. They are superheroes that said, "I can't do this my myself, I need your help."

The most difficult moment for Jose was when he ran his first marathon. The distance was an eternity and he finished in 6 hours and 20 minutes. It was a struggle, but he didn't quit. He made a challenge for himself that the day if he would finish a marathon in 4:30, he would retire from running marathons. He put this time because he saw it impossible, therefore he would never would retire from running. Believe it or not, with the passing of the years, he has improved his time and his PR is 4:33, he says that he is getting close to retirement, but if he breaks that time, he will find another challenge. Jose has read a lot about running and he wants to pass what he learned. He shares his experiences with people that have come to his path, and because of this, we know him as the Professor, "El Profe". Yet, his encouragement is not only with advice. One time, Jose was running with a friend who was running his first marathon. By mile 16, his friend was talking about quitting and taking an Uber. Jose told him that he couldn't give up, that they only have ten more miles to run. Well, he finished just under six hours and he finished without regrets. The regret of not finishing something is worse than the pain of going through.

Wang Deshun, from China, at the age of 79 years old, captivated thousands of people with his energetic and gracious walk on the runway where he was part of a fashion show as a model. It was his debut at the fashion week in China. He was wearing pants with no shirt to let people see his perfect body that easily could be a body of a 30-year-old man. His form and posture were amazing. But it hasn't always had been easy for Wang. In the beginning he was thriving; at the age of 24 he became a theater teacher, at 44 he began learning English, and at 49 he started his own pantomime company. But things started to turn around and times became difficult for Wang. He lost everything and ended up homeless in Beijing. The only had two things in his personal inventory, hope, and determination. He was determined to reinvent himself. At 50, he started going to the gym to take care of his body, and when he was 57, he invented a new form of art of lived sculptures made of people with the entire body painted doing incredible human poses. At 70-years-old, he was fully dedicated to exercise, and then fashion. Wang believes that there are still many dreams of accomplish. It's never too late. If you think you are too old to start something, it's just an excuse. An article from *The New York Times* describes Wang as "China's hottest grandpa"; he has reshaped China's views of aging. Wang was determined to avoid physical and mental stagnation by exploring new skills and ideas. Another habit that I have adopted from Sergio Fernandez is the idea of an island of creativity. You basically take one week a year to write, think of new ideas, and to explore the best ones. Wang says, "One way to tell if you are old or not is to ask yourself, do you dare to try something that you have never done before?" Nature determines age, but you determine your state of mind.

Breaking the Dark Wall

During the Chicago Marathon, I saw people moving away to give way to a couple that was holding a tether. As I approached them, I noticed that one had a shirt marked "Guide" and the other person was a vision impaired runner. I felt such respect for the blind runner; the thought of Hellen Keller came to my mind. I was with such admiration that one person would run 26.2 miles not knowing what was in front of them. I also felt so grateful to the guide that volunteered his time and ran the race to make a dream come true for somebody with limitations. I realize the only limitations are those that we put on ourselves.

If there was somebody that didn't make excuses to run her race, it was Hellen Keller. In her book "The Story of my Life," Hellen Keller describes her autobiography and how she was able to build on her reality to always be better. It is a story of determination and tenacity. Hellen lived in a big house in Alabama and enjoyed the colors, aromas, the sights of flowers and plants of the garden, and the fruits of spring time. But one day things changed. She was just two years old when she got sick with a fever that left her without sight or hearing. Helen grew up with many difficulties. It was frustrating for her and her parents the lack of communication. God sent her an angel. A teacher of the Perkins Institution for the Blind, Ann Sullivan, came to Helen's house and changed her life. Ann taught Hellen to communicate with hand signs. In 1980, Hellen learned to talk by using her hands to feel her lips and tongue to utter words. Finally, she said her first phrase, "It is warm". Helen kept building on her reality to change it. In 1982, she wrote her first story, she went to the Cambridge School for Girls and Radcliffe. She studied many subjects including history of the world and Latin grammar. She later wrote many books. Hellen had a race and it was unique. But she didn't abandon the race. She built her reality and crossed the finish line. Hellen lived in a world or darkness, could not see or hear, she learned to talk but had to use other person to translate the sounds that she made, she was a woman with a great form. Her race was difficult, but she ran it with love and purpose. She ran her race with obstacles, but she stepped up to the challenges. She said, "Life is a daring adventure or nothing." Can you imagine a woman with such limitations saying that life is a daring adventure? That is how we need to see life: like an adventure, a gift from God, and we need to enjoy it and leave a mark in the world around us, in our children and our community. It is our legacy.

He memorized the distance from one goal post to the other goal post at the other side of the soccer field. He went to run at night when nobody was at the field to make sure he wouldn't run into somebody. The distance back and forth was 1.3 miles. Using his run keeper app, he would know when to turn around, what pace to maintain, and the time. Now, he knew the drill, but he wanted to enlarge his territory and would not let his blindness become and obstacle. Simon Wheatcroft, a runner from UK, quit one time in his life because he was blind. But he talked to himself and said, "I'll never quit again." He went outside and pushed the limits of what is possible. That is when he started running. He couldn't be forced to stay within a soccer field. He went to the street with the help of his Run Keeper app and memorized every single turn of the course. He learned where the landmarks were that would indicate where he was at every single moment of his run.

Simon wanted to take the challenge of running solo, so he approached IBM and developed an app with the help of engineers to run in the desert. With innovation and faith, we can find the cracks to tear down the walls. The wall of darkness around Simon, called blindness, was not going to keep him from being free. Technology has allowed Simon and other blind runners to do it by themselves, IBM has the object recognition system. Google has some glasses that connect the runner with people in a room looking on screens what the cameras on the glasses directing the runner of where to go.

He had accidents and it was not an easy task. He bumped into poles, got ran over by cars, but he kept going. He used all his senses to know his position, touching poles, fences, smelling different aromas, counting steps, and running over the painted lines at the side of the road feeling a different texture under his feet while listening the cars go by. It never was easy, but stopping was not an option. The roads that he memorized would take him through the city, the woods, and the open fields for miles and miles. His territory started at the gym, enlarged to a soccer field, then a 3/4 of mile asphalt strip, later to New York and Boston marathons, and finally to 100 miles in the Sahara Desert. There are no limits, there are no excuses.

There are elements you can't control in a race
so focus on those you can!

Photo by Ana Maria Villegas

The one who does not give in, the one who endures, even embraces the pain, is the one who reaches the goal.

Ana Maria Villegas

Photo by Ana Maria Villegas

We get so caught up with material things we forget that the most simple things in life can bring the most happiness.

Chapter 7.
THE FINISH LINE

7 Stars That Became 8

The streets of Caracas were busy. People were running to cross the street giving way to the line of motorcycles that was solid and long and made it difficult for the cars to turn left because they had to break the line. Walking on the sidewalk, Vicky was about to get a 3 and 1 juice from the small juice bar. Beets, oranges and carrots gave a distinct and delicious flavor to the popular juice. That was the final stop for Vicky before she could reach the East Park, where runners meet to train. The park is full of open green grass areas, undulating topography and a beautiful densely forested landscape with pave gardens, murals and lakes, all the while overlooking the magnificent mountain of Avila. She saw long lines waiting at the entrance of the grocery store to get whatever was possible because there was almost nothing to buy. The worthless money could hardly can pay for anything. On her way to the park, Vicky saw a man selling decorations made of money to be used as a souvenir.

Things have changed in Venezuela. The flag doesn't have seven stars anymore; it has eight. A country that was once very rich in natural resources is now living in austerity. With all of these worries, Vicky can't sleep very well; the future of her family is uncertain. But she can't live in the realm of fear. Vicky knows that God is in her side, although it may be difficult to believe when the streets of Caracas are in the dark, without power, and no public transportation or attention at the hospitals is present.

Vicky 's burden is heavy because she is the head of the family. She is lucky to work as a freelancer, selling her services as a web developer to clients all around Latin America. Even though she is getting paid in dollars, what she charges isn't much.

Every time Vicky gets to the park to meet with her friends to go running, she realizes one more person is not showing up because they've decided to leave the country. Some of Vicky's friends live in America and are contributing to make one of Vicky's dream come true: She wants to travel to Chicago for the Marathon in October. Like many others around the world, Vicky put her name in the lottery to see try to get a spot. Guess what? She got it! The news was so great, that she forgot for a moment the pain that she was dealing with every day in Caracas.

When Vicky meets with friends at the park, they have to run in groups because it's dangerous to go running alone, especially for women. Sometimes they have to postpone the training because of raids in the city, but that doesn't stop Vicky from running. Nothing stops her. She started running when she was a girl with her dad, who was a coach. She remembers with great love the days when she was running side-by-side with her father. He started running when he joined the Army at 14 years old. He was kind of shy and didn't talk too much, but when he did, he let his wisdom came out. It came out all the time when he was at court defending cases as a lawyer, but his values conflicted all the time with the corruption and the way things were handled. It created such a pain in his heart to deal with all the wrong things that he decided to leave the legal system.

Vicky's dad enjoyed running and his running time was very valuable. What he enjoyed the most was his time with God, his time with himself, and his time with his daughter. And even though he wasn't a man of many words, his expressions and his look said everything. Sometimes only words are not enough to fully understand somebody's feelings. The nonverbal communication happens unconsciously and spontaneously and can tell more about a person than just words. With his eyes and his hands, he told her how good she was doing, how strong she was, and how beautiful she looked with her long black hair tied in a pony tail that bounced graciously at every stride that she took. Inside of him was a message that needed to come out and it came out beautifully in his poems. His dream was to leave a legacy with his poetry. He decided to write a book and had the determination to do it. It was so good that there is a copy of his book in Washington. He expressed his heart not only with his poems, but with his paintings. His peaceful heart was stamped on canvas and his fighting heart came out through boxing.

Everything was working fine for Vicky's dad, but suddenly things turned around. Unfortunately, he has a health condition and has to take a medicine that is impossible to get in Venezuela. Her friends have made arrangements to send her the medicine. He is still fighting to live. He taught Vicky more than running; he taught her how to fight. Inside of Vicky is a heart of a boxer, a fighter that will run this marathon. The marathon in Chicago and the one back home every day in the ring that destiny has brought to Vicky and many others in Venezuela.

The empty streets of Caracas are transformed when Vicky and her running group take over. The group, besides being a way to deal with the insecurity, has found a way to get energy from others. Caracas is one of the most dangerous cities in the world with 122 homicides for every 100,000 habitants. "Runners Venezuela" is

Vicky's group, and for her and the others in the group, is the outlet from being tired of not being able to do exercise due to the insecurity. There are about 300 to 350 runners that meet to share the roads of Caracas. Every week they meet, not only to run, but to do yoga and Pilates. It's really a way to have a break from the political situation of the country and from all those feelings of worry, fear, and anxiety.

Finally, the day came. Vicky was heading to Maiquetia International Airport. Thanks to her friends, she was able to get some money because the Bolivar is impossible to exchange money. The airport looked empty. There was nothing on the shelves of the duty-free stores. But it was time to board the plane! Once the plane was on the air, Vicky looked through the window at the beautiful hill next to the water, thinking that the next time she was going to see that hill, it will be with her Chicago Marathon medal hanging from her neck. A medal that she is going to show to her children and will bring to the Wednesday's night run with the "Runners Venezuela" to show her friends and to thank them for their help during the training.

After a series of long hours flying and airplane changes, Vicky could see the Willis Tower, the most iconic building in Chicago, from the window. Also known as the Sears Tower, it's one of the tallest buildings in the USA. Such a monumental architectural structure that was conceived in the mind of a man that came with the idea when he played with cigarettes. Putting them together at different heights gave him the idea for the design of the tower. The same power in the mind of the architect Fazlur Rahman Khan who was born in Bangladesh, is the power of the mind that is going to let Vicky run her first international marathon.

Vicky looked down at the glass floor that was build out of the structure on the open air for people to take pictures. She noticed a couple or runners, a husband and a wife. What caught the attention of Vicky was that the husband was blind. She couldn't resist the temptation to talk to them and asked if they were going to run the marathon. When Vicky learned the story of the blind runner, she thought to herself: What an encouragement, a man that couldn't see, but let his heart come out in running. She taught about her dad, a man that couldn't talked very much, but let his heart come out in his running, poems, paintings, and his daughter.

She looked at the route that was going to take her through the marathon. She closed her fist and lifted her arm saying, "I am going to do it, I am going to run for my dad, I am going to run for my kids, and I am going to run for my country. And when I cross the finish line, I am going to lift the yellow, blue, and red flag with seven stars and I am going to yield, 'Arriba Venezuela, si podemos.'"

Smile at the Bad Weather

Like Vicky, in the past story, this is also a non-fictitious story of a runner this time from Fort Lauderdale. Vince enjoys running and always makes good things from bad things. Everything works for Vince. One time, he was running the Fort Lauderdale A1A marathon. The people in front started with a very good and strong pace and got separated from the main group for less than one mile. Vince and the runners that were with him tried to catch up, but they saw the bars coming down the street when a train was approaching. They tried to increase the pace, but couldn't make it, the train got there first. They couldn't believe what was going on; the race was broken in two by a train. Everybody was complaining and rubbing their head in disbelief. But Vince said, "You know, at least I can regain my strength and do the second half stronger." I don't know how the organization was able to stop the time for those left behind and restart as soon as the train was gone, but at the end, Vince was able to keep his time.

Great news for Vince, he won the lottery to enter the Chicago Marathon. He prepared very well for about 18 weeks, with days of running in the heat, humidity and rainy days of South Florida. Finally, the day arrived. He tied his colorful shoes made for stability, headed out for the airport, and thought that if his baggage was going to get lost, at least he could keep his shoes. That's exactly what happened. The weather was good on the way to the airport and he had some time to kill before departure time. He was tired and fell sleep in the waiting room. When he woke up, he didn't see anybody at the gate and panic started to move in. He ran to the counter and the lady told him that his flight was moved to another gate. Running in the airport, Vince rushed to the new gate. The entire time he was rubbing his head. When he got to the gate, he could watch the door closing as he was approaching. He lost the flight – what a bummer!

Now Vince had to wait for a new flight, but nothing was going out until the next day, so the airline decided to put him in a hotel. In the least, he thought it was nice for the airline gave him a toiletry bag and that he got a free night in a nice hotel.

The next day came and Vince finally arrived in Chicago. He went straight to the Sears Tower to take a look of the city that was hosting this big race for him, and for 45,000 other runners. He was excited to see from the window the beautiful city and got to take some pictures with other runners; There was a runner that came from Venezuela and a mom that came from Miami and a runner that came from Colombia.

The day of the race was cold and rainy. People were complaining about it, but for Vince, it was the perfect temperature. He smiled at the bad weather and thought, "It is what it is." But "it is what it is" can be different depending on how you see it. In the movie Life is Beautiful, "La Vita è Bella", Guido is a person that sees things from different angles. But that view was tested to the extreme when World War II broke out in Europe. He fell in love with Dora and set up "confidential" incidents to show his affection for Dora until she gave in to him. Dora was engaged to another man, an arrogant man, and in her engagement party, Guido steals her and runs away on a horse. Eventually, they got married and have a son, Guiosuè.

Guido, his son, and his uncle were taken and sent to a concentration camp. His uncle was executed in a gas chamber. Guido knew the severity of the situation that he was with his son, but chose to do the impossible to make his son believe that everything they went through was a game. I am not saying that we have to look at things like they are a game, but we can choose how to react to situations and make the complicated ones simpler.

In moments when their lives were in danger, Guido convinced his son that they are in middle of a "hide and seek" game; he sheltered his son from the horror of the camp. Things got more tense as the allies approached the concentration camp and the German soldiers tried to exterminate as many Jews as they could. Guido managed to keep his son hidden in a box as "part of the game". They had to run from hidden place to hidden place, but Guido was taken to be executed. He was able to glance for last time at his son and chose to wink at him, making him believe that he was still in the middle of the game. Guido was shot and left dead in an alleyway. The prize that Guido told his son for winning the game was a tank. The next day after Guido was executed, Guosuè emerged from the box where he was hiding when he heard an American soldier liberating the camp. Nobody was left except Guiosuè. He was taken to the tank with the American soldier to liberty. He won the game and the prize of a tank. Guido lost the game and he went through utter horror, but decided to make his son look at things differently to keep him alive.

Vince also looked at things differently. Many unexpected things happened to him, but he smiled at the bad weather. Now, he is in his corral ready to start his marathon in Chicago. It is cold, it is raining, it is windy, but he is happy to be there. He enjoys being with other people that have come a long way to be there. He is ready to start next to a Venezuelan girl named Vicky, a mom from Miami named Martha, a blind runner and his wife, and a guide. He is enjoying the beautifully bad weather. He is enjoying the last days of his life and accomplishing his dreams. The doctor gave him no more than six months to live and cancer wanted to finish Vince's race short. But for Vince, every minute is precious because "La Vita è Bella".

Give Me A Break

It's getting late and Martha is coming back home from a long day at her job at the publishing company. Her office on the 13th floor has a huge window with a beautiful view of downtown Miami and the MacArthur Causeway. She stared outside and looked at the route that was going to take her over the bridge and back as she reviewed her training plan on her cell phone.

Martha has been running since she was 16. In high school she joined the track team. She looked forward to the competitions and the interaction with the team. Running definitely was part of her life. After she graduated, she met her boyfriend in college. When they got together, they joined the running club to train and travel to different races. She was in shape, she felt full of energy, and running was the one thing that she enjoyed the most. Is was her time expanding her relationship with God. When she started the run of the day, she went through a warm up. Her pace was with some effort, but then she started to feel her tempo, she heard her breathing, she felt like being in auto pilot. She was inundated with praise and thankfulness in her heart.

Martha had ran several marathons, all with something special for her. But when she was getting ready for a Boston qualifying race, she got pregnant. With the twins' arrival, things were different. In the beginning it was hard to manage the load, and it got harder. There were nights with few hours of sleep only to head to work. She'd have to find a place to pump milk and save it to bring it home, shores, doctors' appointments, with no time for her. It got so difficult that she started to have mixed feelings towards the twins. She loved them, but she didn't look forward to the time with them. It was demanding and draining all her energy. She started getting some signs of depression and was hard for her even to do her basic activities.

She was in a constant rush and lacked focus. When she was at work, she thought about the twins all the time, and when she was with the twins, she thought about work all the time. It was difficult for her to be present in the moment. Sometimes when she would bring work problems, home, and home problems to work. It was a constant balance.

Martha was able to find a place for herself. The quiet time was at three in the morning, in the presence of God; she felt like she was by a river of living water. Her spirit got stronger, her body got stronger after starting to eat better, and since her bulimia was under control, the table was in balance. Now she wanted the place in the outdoors, a place open for creation. She wanted to hit the asphalt and let the blood circulate in her brain and her heart to pump hard.

With the twins older, and her husband covering the 4:00 am shift, Martha finally hit the asphalt. Her shoes were tied, her watch was charged, and her friends were waiting for her at the track. Today she was going to do speed work. Wow, only three more weeks for Chicago. Her challenge, her goal. This is her own space; this is her own time where she didn't have to think about the twins or work.

The time came for Martha to leave for Chicago and she left her husband to take care of the twins. When she kissed them goodbye, she looked at their blue eyes and she said, "You are beautiful, you have something special and unique, and one day your dreams will become true, like my dream is coming true in Chicago." That moment became a memory. The images of the twins were in Martha's head during the trip to Chicago, and during the marathon when she was running, she felt like giving up. She saw the twins' faces and kept repeating, "You have unique, you have dreams, and they will come true, like my dream is coming true. Chicago is waiting for me, and I am going to see my dream come true."

When Martha arrived in Chicago, she went for a walk and went to the Sears Tower. She met a couple that was running the marathon. He was blind and his wife was going to be his guide for the race. She also met a single mom from Venezuela and a man from Fort Lauderdale that barely make it to the attraction. From the expo, she went to the hotel. She got settled, put on her gear on the bed for the next day of the race, and before going to bed, she gave thanks; thanks for being in Chicago, thanks for the twins, for her job, and for the people that she met in the tower. The table was not going to fall since everything was in balance. There was so much to be grateful for!

I See You

By now you can see I like movies. There is another movie called "Avatar". The people of Pandora had a greeting, "I see you". It was used to show when they could see through the eyes and into the deep soul. Through that veil, they discovered what the heart of the other person really looked like.

In this story, Tony is sitting in the airplane next to his wife, Jessica. She is describing to him the deep blue sky and the how the sun was shining on the islands, where they just spent their honeymoon. She described the view to him because Tony is blind. He lost his vision ten years ago in a military operation when he got hit by a bullet. He was carried in a medevac helicopter to a base hospital and was plugged in to a machine. For days, Tony couldn't talk due to the recovery, but when they doctor took his bandages away and he realized that the world looked blurry and different, he went silent for weeks. The old, energetic, and happy Tony wasn't there anymore. Tony didn't want to be that way, though. He wanted to be himself again. He wanted his life to be a daring adventure, like Helen Keller said.

When Tony returned home, the post-conflict trauma, plus his new condition, took a toll. But Tony renewed his mind and he set goals for himself. He wanted to train for running. He started running on a treadmill, holding the bars with his hands. Then he let them go and started running with his hands free. After he mastered running on the treadmill, but he wanted to go outside. Initially, he started running on the track with his dog Tux, a border collie, that looks like he was always wearing a tuxedo suit. Eventually, he found other runners that would go with him. He felt free and rejuvenated. He enjoyed running so much that he decided to join a race. But he didn't know what to do since Tux couldn't go to the race with him. Somebody told him how to find a running guide; together they explored Running Eyes on the internet and he found an angel.

Help was on the way; his guide was Jessica. They started running together, holding a tether. Jessica started training with Tony and would give clues of any changes in terrain or of turns to take. After the first race, they synchronized their pace and were running at the same tempo. They synchronized their heart and felt in love. Approaching the finish line, they started dancing and laughing and enjoying each other. Finally, Tony was the same he was before. Tony, with a heart full of joy, told Jessica, "I see you; I see you, Jessica." He saw her through the veil of her heart and saw who Jessica really was.

When Tony and Jessica arrived in Chicago, they went to the Sears Tower. Jessica described how the city looked, and how the rivers, streets, and parks looked that they were going to pass during their race. They thought about the new challenge and their goal. They saw themselves as warriors and as they listen the stories of people around them talking about their race. They met a girl from Venezuela that was fighting for her dreams and the dreams of her children. One man was fighting to spend the last days of his life the best way he could. Each runner in the race was going to take place the next day had his or her own story. The goal was much more than run 26.2 miles, yet the 26.2 miles was part of the whole thing, the real race.

The Most Beautiful Race

Life is not a sprint, it is like a marathon with many curves, ups, and downs. The real race is really a short distance race. It is a race where somebody can make it to the next mailbox, and from there, onto the another. The real race is like compound interest, we go little by little, one step at a time. We accomplish our goals with a series of small goals. We live our years and our months based on how we live in our present day. It's in this moment and how can we prepare for the moment after this. We accomplish things with baby steps and we eat an elephant one bite at a time. We worry about the present and tomorrow will have its own worry. Our lives will be more fulfilling if we live this day as if it's the last day of our lives.

Starting in Chicago, the runners quickly tried to go to the bathroom for the last time before the race started. Vicky pushed her way forward to get on time to her corral and found a place in the crowd to start the race. She looked around and recognized Vince, Martha, Jessica, Tony from the day before at the Sears Tower. She gave them a high five, all with the starting with the culmination of a dream that came true. The light rain was the background for a beautiful rainbow. As the runners started the course, they had to go around the puddles but they came to a street that was shining with sun. With every strike of their feet, a splash of water was leaving the edges of their shoes. For an instant, it looked like the runners were running on water.

That's actually where the most beautiful race took place: over the water. It was not a marathon; it was a 100 meters race. It was not running, it was walking. The race took place on a lake, about 2,000 years ago, where only one runner was in the race. His name was Peter. The wind was strong, the sky was dark grey, and the waves were big. The runner was on a boat like many times before. He knew every single inch of the boat. It was his life. He lived from the lake as a fisherman. He had been many times in rough waters, but never in the middle of a storm like this. In that moment, he found himself afraid of what could happen.

For the first time in his life, he felt that he didn't have everything under control. In the middle of the storm he heard a voice saying, "Peter, come." It was like somebody was saying, "On your marks, get set, go!" The race began! He was afraid of making his first step. He took his foot out of the boat and into the unknown over the water. "I am going to drown," he said, "But what can I lose. There is nothing left to lose." He believed, and let his body go. He didn't sink and he didn't drown. Something was holding him, so he took his second foot out of the boat. He stepped out of his comfort zone, out of his security, put all his being in what was holding him, and started his 100 meters race. The sky opened, the clouds moved to reveal the sun shine, and the waters where calm. The rainbow came and it looked like the street of Chicago, were Vicky, Vince, Martha, Jessica and Tony, we're running. He fell one time when he took his eyes from God, but he got up. God's hands were there to pull him from the hole and to hold him. He pushed forward and completed the race to the finish line, to the medal, and to the reward; the reward was God himself. His love and presence surrounded him and he felt the hug of God, his arms around him, embracing him with love. His beautiful voice said, "You made it. I got you, I got you. Don't worry, everything will be ok."

Sometimes we have things under control, we plan, we act, we see results, and life is good. We have been in the same boat for long time. But a storm can come our way and it can be a storm like we have never seen before. We might find ourselves in a place where we don't know what to do or where to go. We might listen to the advice people can offer to us, but things might look like they won't work, and we might find ourselves alone where there is not hope. In the middle of the storm, is where the real race starts. The 100 meters walking over the water race.

The runner of the most beautiful race was in his boat. The other people on the boat were too scared to move. They were paralyzed. In this time of despair, he heard something. He heard his name from the distance, from 100 meters away, and that seemed like 1,000 meters because of the storm. He heard his name, "Peter, Peter come!" It was the voice of God calling him by his name, because He knew Peter's name. He also knows your name. He knows the wrinkle on your cheeks when you smile, your freckles, the color of your eyes, the tears that are falling from your eyes, and the steps that you are taking. He knows your thoughts, your dreams, your problems, and your feelings. He knows everything about you.

The sun shined through the rain. As the rainbow was rising, Martha, Vince, Vicky, Jessica and Tony, found themselves alone again, running against themselves. Pushing their way through, they had mixed feelings and thoughts. What is going to happen after, what is going to happen to the twins, to the family, to the country, to the health, to the job that is not coming. But God knows their name, he knows who Martha is, who Vince is, and who Vicky is.

The most beautiful race is the one you are doing right now. I don't know if you just started, if you are in mile 5, mile 12, or mile 26. All I know is that in the next 100 meters, you will be ready for the following 100 meters, and the next, and that you are not alone. God knows your name, he is calling you by your name, He cares for you, loves you, and wants the best for you. Put your eyes on the prize, keep your eyes on Jesus and you won't sink.

You can cross the finish line and you can hear the one calling you by your name saying, "You made it, well done!" I want to congratulate you for all those times that you have being a blessing to others, sharing tips, running alongside them, waiting for somebody, giving a hug, pitching in for a cause, giving your smile away, and making this a better place. Well done! I say to you, well done! But it won't be anything compared to the time when you hear it from God. So, open your ears, open your heart, and have faith that you can hear that voice.

Well done my friend, we can do this! We'll get our reward, we'll cross the finish line!

WORKS CITED

1. Keller, G. (n.d.). Papasan, J. (2013). *The One Thing: The Surprisingly Simple Truth Behind Extraordinary Results.* Bard Press.

2. Dr. Maffetone, P. (2000). *The Maffetone Method. The Holistic, No stress, No-pain Way to Exceptional Fitness.* Ragged Mountain Press.

3. Bunyan, J. (1967). *The pilgrim's progress.* Grand Rapids: Zondervan Pub. House.

4. Biography.com (2019) *Ben Carson Biography.* A (PBS Digital Studios, 2016)&E Television Networks. https://www.biography.com/political-figure/ben-carson

5. Burke, Louise & M. Castell, Linda & Casa, Douglas & Close, Graeme & Costa, Ricardo & Desbrow, Ben & Halson, Shona & Lis, Dana & Melin, Anna & Peeling, Peter & U. Saunders, Philo & Slater, Gary & Sygo, Jennifer & C. Witard, Oliver & Bermon, Stéphane & Stellingwerff, Trent. (2019). International Association of Athletics Federations Consensus Statement 2019: *Nutrition for Athletics. International Journal of Sport Nutrition and Exercise Metabolism.* 29. 1-12. 10.1123/ijsnem.2019-0065.

6. Dr. Leaf, C. (2019). *The Perfect You. A Blueprint for Identity.* Ada. Baker Publishing Company.

7. Dr. Leaf, C. (2009). *Who Switched Off my Brain?* Southlake. Inprov Limited

8. Dr. Ratey, J and Hagerman, E. (2012) *SPARK! How Exercise Will Improve the Performance of Your Brain.* London. Quercus Publishing.

9. Proathleteadvantage.com (2019). *6 Time Ironman Champ Mark Allen Shares How to Be Fearless in the Face of Your Fears.* https://www.proathleteadvantage.com/Face-your-fears-with-mark-allen

10. Pbs.org (2016). *Science of Marathon Running.* https://www.pbs.org/video its-okay-be-smart-marathon/

11. Therunexperience.com (2017). *Proper Running Footstrike: 3 Steps to Improve it!* https://therunexperience.com/proper-running-footstrike-3-steps-to-improve-it/

12. Tappan, T. and Roth, D. (1983). *Love Isn't Love (Til You Give it Away). Performed by Reba McEntire.* Nashville.

13. Lapin, D. (2014) *Business Secrets from the Bible: Spiritual Success Strategies for Financial Abundance.* Wiley

14. McCaw, S. (2014). *Biomechanics For Dummies.* Hoboken. John Wiley & Sons, Inc.

15. Williams, K Ph. D (1985) *Biomechanics of Running.* Exercise and Sport Science Reviews. Volume 13- Issue 1- ppg 389-442

16. Therunexperience.com (2019). *How to Increase Running Stamina with 6 Simple Tips* https://therunexperience.com how-to-increase-running-stamina-with-6-simple-tips/

17. Galloway, J. (1984) *Galloway.s Book on Running.* Bolinas. Shelter Publications

18. Saunders, P. (2004) *Factors affecting running economy in trained distance runners.* sports Med. 34 (7) 465-85

19. Howard, B. & Moore, R. (2016) *Zootopia.* Walt Disney Pictures

20.   Runnersworld.com. Cathal, D. (2016) *The Simple Life of One of the World's Best Marathoners*. https://www.runnersworld.com/news/a20793538/the-simple-life-of-one-of-the-worlds-best-marathoners/

21.   Nike.com (2019) *Breaking2: The Documentary*. Nike. *https://www.nike.com us/en_us/c/running/breaking2*

22.   Firstpost.com (2012) *Irish missionary at heart of Kenya's running mecca.* https://www.firstpost.com/sports/irish-missionary-at-heart-of-kenyas-running-mecca-384710.html

23.   Therunexperience.com (2014) *Feature on Competitor: Fix Two Common Running Form Flaws.* https://therunexperience.com/featured-on-competitor-fixing-two-common-running-form-flaws/

24.   Active.com (2019) *10 Best Running Cities in the U.S. https://www.active.com running/articles/10-best-running-cities-in-the-u-s*

25.   Strayer.com (2014) *What Success Means to Americans (Infographic).* Buzz. https://www.strayer.edu/buzz/what-success-means-americans-infographic

26.   Melrobbins.com (2019) *10 Questions to help you visualize your future.* https:/melrobbins.com/blog/10-questions-to-help-you-visualize-your-future/

27.   Prestatupierna.org (2019) https://www.prestatupierna.org

Well done, we can do this

We can cross the finish line.

Photo by Luis Tovar

You are not what you achieve, you are what you overcome.

Ana Maria Villegas

Photo by Ana Maria Villegas